RONALD KNOX AS APOLOGIST

FATHER MILTON T. WALSH

Ronald Knox as Apologist: Wit, Laughter and the Popish Creed

IGNATIUS PRESS   SAN FRANCISCO

Biblical citations are taken from Ronald Knox' translation of the Holy Bible.

The Knox Brothers by Penelope Fitzgerald, © 1977, 2000 has been reprinted by permission of HarperCollins Publishers Ltd. and by permission of Counterpoint Press, a member of Perseus Books, L.L.C.

Front cover photograph:
Ronald Arbuthnott Knox
by Howard Coster
National Portrait Gallery, London

Cover design by Roxanne Mei Lum

Mary of Holyrood may smile indeed,
Knowing what grim historic shade it shocks
To see wit, laughter and the Popish creed
Cluster and sparkle in the name of Knox.

CONTENTS

PREFACE

When Evelyn Waugh produced a collection of sermons by his friend, he trumpeted the preacher's prominence in the title: *A Selection from the Occasional Sermons of the Right Reverend Monsignor Ronald Arbuthnott Knox; sometime Scholar of Balliol College and Fellow of Trinity College, Oxford; Domestic Prelate to His Holiness the Pope*. One can picture the learned prelate sipping a sherry with the Marchmains at Brideshead. Yet with all of these distinctions, most people knew him as "Ronald Knox", and for a great many he was simply "Ronnie".

Throughout the first half of the twentieth century, as both an Anglican and a Roman Catholic, Ronald Knox was a part of the English landscape. He was the favored preacher for occasions great and small; his articles on a host of general topics found a place in the Sunday newspapers and monthly literary magazines; his voice was often heard on the BBC. Most significant was the tide of books that flowed from his pen, which found wide readership both in Great Britain and abroad.

He expressed himself in a remarkable variety of genres: from limericks and detective stories to belles-lettres and spiritual conferences. He was a humanist and a Christian, who could employ his considerable talents to translate the Bible or take the reader on a tour of Trollope's Barchester. He could grapple with profound philosophical and theological issues, and he could write for fun. He could amuse, edify, or challenge—and not infrequently, he did all three in the same work.

But if Ronald Knox was a writer by temperament, he was a priest by vocation; writing was the chosen tool of his apostolate. Throughout his life, Knox devoted his energies principally to sharing the truth of the Christian faith as he understood it. No theologian, in his apologetical writings, conferences, and sermons he did not seek innovation. If his contemporary C. S. Lewis sought to present "mere Christianity", Knox—both as an Anglican and after his conversion—described "mere Catholicism". Mere, not in the sense of minimal, but in the sense that his was not the theology of a party or a school, but simply "the mind of the Church".

The immense popularity of his religious books with a wide public testifies to his effectiveness. Readers found in Ronald Knox a man who was able to combine intellectual rigor and religious engagement, a priest who could present the faith with conviction but who could sympathize with the difficulties others faced. Even after his untimely death in 1957, the tide flowed on: several of his retreat conferences and essays were published posthumously. Those who would never hear him speak could still be instructed and edified by his insights.

In the years following the Second Vatican Council, this once familiar figure went into eclipse. His translation of the Vulgate Bible was set aside, as new translations from the original Hebrew and Greek became available. In the ecumenical euphoria following the Council, many felt that an author who argued—albeit persuasively—for the unique claims of Catholicism was passé. Many Catholics rejected what they viewed as an excessively intellectual popular approach to the faith before the Council. Knox, as we shall see, would have had some sympathy with their position, but as a proponent of the preconciliar approach, Monsignor Knox' day was over. By a curious historical amnesia, people seemed to assume that nothing of much value had happened between the end of the New Testament and the year 1965.

There are signs that the eclipse may be passing. Some of Ronald Knox' books that had gone out of print are again seeing the light of day. More generally, there is a greater interest in apologetics today than there was twenty or thirty years ago. There are several reasons for this. The first might be described as the principle of youthful revolution: if one generation leads a revolt against *The Baltimore Catechism*, it should come as no surprise that the next generation rises up against the reduction of catechesis to making collages. And, more so than in the past, practicing Catholics today need answers on hand "if anyone asks [them] to give an account of the hope which [they] cherish" (1 Pet 3:15). Until recently, most Christians could be carried along in the stream of a culture which, if it did not espouse Christian beliefs, at least honored them. Today the situation is very different: anyone who professes Christian faith is swimming against a very powerful stream, and Catholics more so than others.

We Catholics may be less aware of our predicament than many Protestants; they have been wrestling for a century with challenges we have confronted only in the last forty years. As in Knox' lifetime, so today it is often converts who value the treasures of faith that cradle Catholics take for granted. As one of the most significant convert writers of the twentieth century, Knox stands with G. K. Chesterton and others as a guide to those treasures.

But isn't Ronald Knox out of date? Let us consider challenges Catholics face today; a perusal of the "Religion" section of a general bookstore reveals some of them. There we find a spate of books churned out by the proponents of "the Jesus Seminar" and their kind that promise to give us "the real Jesus" unencumbered by the dogmatic accretions of the Church. Such books are touted as "revolutionary" and "ground-breaking"—but in fact, their authors are simply recycling positions advanced a century ago. Back then, some learned scholars sought to approach the Bible solely through literary means, and to read it without the "prejudices" of faith. As both an Anglican and a Catholic, Knox resolutely opposed such an enterprise, and he can lead us through the same thicket of intellectual pretensions today. And one can only imagine what sport he would make of the bizarre fantasy that Jesus faked his crucifixion and settled down with Mary Magdalen in the south of France!

Is he "unecumenical"? He certainly was convinced that in the Catholic faith is to be found the fullness of the truth Christ came to reveal to mankind. That conviction led him through the crucible of conversion, which created a painful chasm between him and those whom he most loved in this world. However, the gulf created by intellectual conviction was bridged by human affection; he cared passionately about the truth, but at the same time he knew that other people, no less virtuous or astute than himself, did not agree with him about where the truth was to be found. None of his gifted brothers shared his Catholic faith—indeed, one of them was an atheist—and yet the four Knox brothers were inseparable. Ronald Knox could sympathize with those who did not see things as he did; he could identify where Catholics held beliefs in common with other Christians; and he could present the case for the Catholic position with clarity and feeling. This is precisely the kind of ecumenism the Second Vatican Council called for.

The purpose of this book is to take down from the shelf those writings by Ronald Knox that can be described broadly as "apologetic". This includes not only books in which he presents a rationale for the Catholic faith to those who do not hold it, but also many of his conferences and sermons addressed to Catholics, in which he seeks to help them better understand the faith they do hold. As much as possible, we will let Ronald Knox speak for himself, because part of his genius lies not only in what he said, but how he said it.

Knox pictured the teaching Church, not as some harassed official handing out information at a series of press conferences, but as a patient pioneer panning for gold. For two thousand years, she has invited us to seek with her the gold of God's wisdom. Prospecting is demanding work: the seeker must travel to unexplored places, endure privations, and carefully discriminate between true ore and "fool's gold". Such an undertaking is more pleasant when carried out with a companion, and Ronald Knox is good company indeed.

ABBREVIATIONS OF
WORKS BY RONALD KNOX
FREQUENTLY CITED IN THIS BOOK

BC   *The Belief of Catholics.* 4th ed. London and New York: Sheed and Ward, 1953. First published in 1927 by Ernest Benn.

CSM   *The Creed in Slow Motion.* New York: Sheed and Ward, 1949.

Dif   *Difficulties: Being a Correspondence about the Catholic Religion between Ronald Knox and Arnold Lunn.* A new edition with two additional letters in conclusion. London: Eyre and Spottiswoode, 1952.

GA   *God and the Atom.* London: Sheed and Ward, 1945.

OR   *Off the Record.* New York: Sheed and Ward, 1954.

OS   *The Occasional Sermons of Ronald A. Knox.* Edited with an introduction by Philip Caraman. London: Burns and Oates; New York: Sheed and Ward, 1960.

PGNA   *Proving God: A New Apologetic.* With a preface by Evelyn Waugh. London: *The Month,* 1959.

PS   *Pastoral Sermons of Ronald A. Knox.* Edited with an introduction by Philip Caraman. London: Burns Oates and Washbourne; New York: Sheed and Ward, 1960.

SA   *A Spiritual Aeneid.* New York: Sheed and Ward, 1958. Reprint of the 1950 edition, with an added preface by Evelyn Waugh. First published in 1918 by Longmans, Green, London. New ed. with a preface "After 33 Years" published in 1950 by Burns Oates and Washbourne, London.

SLS   *Some Loose Stones: Being a Consideration of Certain Tendencies in Modern Theology, Illustrated by Reference to the Book called "Foundations".* London: Longmans, Green, 1913.

US   *University Sermons of Ronald A. Knox, Together with Sermons Preached on Various Occasions.* Edited with an introduction by Philip Caraman. London: Burns Oates and Washbourne; New York: Sheed and Ward, 1963.

PART ONE

SEEKING THE TREASURE: APOLOGETICS IN THE LIFE OF RONALD KNOX

BEFORE CONVERSION
(1888–1915)

Ronald Knox was born on February 17, 1888, the youngest of six children in a strongly Evangelical Anglican family; his ancestors had been Presbyterians. By the time of his ordination in 1912, Knox had emerged as one of the most prominent leaders of the Anglo-Catholic movement; by 1915 he was struggling to maintain his allegiance to the Church of England.

Ronald grew up "in the manse": both his grandfathers had been clergymen, and his father, Edmund A. Knox, was appointed Bishop of Manchester during Ronald's youth. Bishop Knox was strongly committed to the Evangelical wing of the Church of England; he resolutely opposed the ritualism of the Oxford Movement and dismissed Newman as "a misguided weakling".[1] Evangelical Christianity was the religion of Ronald's childhood, and in his *Spiritual Aeneid*,[2] Knox described its basic tenets: the personal love of God, the miracle of redemption, and easy access to the Savior (*SA*, 6). Ronald's mother died when he was four, and he and his brother Wilfred stayed for periods of time

---

[1] Penelope Fitzgerald, *The Knox Brothers* (London: Macmillan, 1977), p. 99.

[2] Ronald Knox, *A Spiritual Aeneid* (1918; New York: Sheed and Ward, 1958); hereinafter, *SA*.

with various relatives. From these relatives, later from his step-mother, and above all from his father, Ronald Knox learned the lesson of holiness from example—and for the rest of his life, he would be marked by a thirst for sanctity and conformity to God's will.

Even against the high standards of his talented family, Ronald's abilities stood out early:

> As for Ronnie, the little boy who had been asked at four years old what he liked doing and he had replied, "I think all day, and at night I think about the past", was already a natural philosopher. He made a docile and friendly pupil, saved from any temptation to vanity by his relentless elder brothers.[3]

As a "natural philosopher" he exhibited an early interest in the powers of logic. In fact, Penelope Fitzgerald traces its importance back to the very first book Ronald owned as a boy, J. C. Wood's *Natural History*:

> "It were an easy task to prove the unity of mankind by scriptural proofs," Wood wrote in his introduction, "but I thought it better to use rational arguments." This went deep. Ronnie told Eddie that there were "rational arguments" why he should be allowed to join the brothers' inner group—the St. Philip's Pioneering and Military Tramway Society; they were not accepted, he had to pass the set tests, but Ronnie remained convinced of the supreme saving power of reason.[4]

Throughout his life, Ronald Knox would advance "rational arguments" to explain his faith.

But the precocious boy who sought to map the philosophical highway of "the True" did not neglect the winding path of "the Beautiful". At the age of six, he began writing hymns—". . . but I am afraid, from what I can re-

---

[3] Fitzgerald, *Knox Brothers*, p. 46.
[4] Fitzgerald, *Knox Brothers*, p. 51.

member, that my efforts were deeply indebted to the work of previous authors" (*SA,* 14)—poetry, and plays. It was at Eton that this affective side of Ronald Knox blossomed:

> The romantic in him, the inconvenient love of mystery and beauty—inconvenient that is, to one who thought he mistrusted enthusiasm and only valued a reasonable faith—began to spread its wings. He felt a devotion to Henry VI, the Sorrowful King, the Founder of Eton, which merged, in this thirteenth year, with his feeling for the poetry of the Rossettis and for the splendour of the west window of St. Philip's, the Burne-Jones window through whose ruby-red glass the light streamed in at evensong.[5]

In his *Spiritual Aeneid*, Knox wrote of this attraction to the Pre-Raphaelite poets, the Gothic Revival, as well as of a fondness for Browning and Keats (*SA,* 35–36). To these, he later added an interest in the seventeenth-century Metaphysical Poets, especially Herbert Vaughan.

It was from this "romantic" angle that Ronald Knox first established contact with the Catholic expression of Christian faith. True to his Evangelical upbringing, he could isolate the moment of his conversion: it took place on Christmas Day, 1903, when he read R. H. Benson's *The Light Invisible* (*SA,* 31). This book helped Knox make a connection between the romance of the Gothic and the religious conviction of his Evangelical childhood.

If Benson's book allowed Knox to get his feet wet in the stream of Anglo-Catholicism, it was another book that enticed him to dive in. In 1904, he read a sympathetic study of the Oxford Movement, Wakefield's *History of the Church of England*. This struck another chord from childhood—an enthusiasm for lost causes:

[5] Fitzgerald, *Knox Brothers*, p. 57.

> I read, and was carried off my feet; I lived through the early
> struggles, followed breathlessly the story of *Tracts for the Times*,
> trembled for Newman, mourned for him as lost to the Church,
> and rose with the knowledge that somewhere, beyond the cir-
> cles I moved in, there was a Cause for which clergymen had
> been sent to prison, a Bishop censured, noble lives spent; a
> Cause which could be mine (*SA,* 33).

That Ronald Knox should want to become a clergyman
surprised no one; both by background and aptitude he was
well-suited for a career in the Church. But the direction he
was taking in this regard was not one of which his father ap-
proved. The bishop's son began to adopt ascetical practices,
and, in order to be completely available for God's service,
he made a private vow of celibacy at the age of seventeen.

   Throughout Knox' life—and in his apologetics—there is
a tension between the rational and the affective. Both elements are always present, vying for center stage. Whereas at
Eton, it was the affective that predominated, the advantage
went to the rational when Knox left Eton for Oxford and
Balliol. His cleverness, his command of English, and his intellectual gifts soon established his reputation as a debater.

> I was early marked down for a speaker who could be depended
> upon to support any view in a debating society. . . . I must
> have acquired an unenviable reputation for defending the in-
> defensible. . . . I have once, owing to a shortage of speakers,
> opened and opposed the same motion.[6]

In later life, Ronald Knox questioned the value of these de-
bates: he felt they trained a speaker to avoid the obvious and
search for the ingenious. He attributed his delay in embrac-

---

[6] Quoted in Evelyn Waugh, *Monsignor Ronald Knox* (Boston and Toronto:
Little, Brown, 1959), p. 93; source not given.

ing Roman Catholicism partly to the fact that "it seemed so obvious".[7]

Knox' talents brought him not only forensic victories but academic ones as well. He took a first in "Greats", the examination on Roman and Greek history and philosophy, which marked an important stage in his intellectual growth:

> A first in Greats left me neither a professional philosopher nor a professional historian; but it left me with a fierce love of sifting evidence and the power of not being fascinated into acquiescence when superior persons talked philosophy at me (*SA*, 55).

Yet even as he was excelling in his studies, Knox came to think of the supernatural order as something to which reason was not the key any more than feeling; the "Absolute" of the philosophers was a neuter object, not the God he loved and worshipped (*SA*, 54).

During this time, Ronald Knox continued in his Anglo-Catholic direction: he frequented Pusey House, made retreats with the Anglican monks on Caldey Island, and grew in his devotion to the Reserved Sacrament. He also visited Belgium, where the piety of the people made a deep impression on him. Before his Anglo-Catholic days, Knox had visited Rome with his brothers but was oblivious to its religious aspect. Now, as a Ritualist, he was deeply moved by a culture where Catholicism was a daily reality: in the words of Evelyn Waugh, "Flemish quaintness moved him where Roman magnificence had failed."[8]

In 1910, Knox moved from Balliol to Trinity College and began his studies for ordination. Neither at this time nor later when he was preparing for the Roman Catholic

[7] Ibid., p. 93.
[8] Waugh, *Monsignor Ronald Knox*, p. 104.

priesthood did Knox follow a set course of studies; because
of his intellectual gifts he was given the freedom to con-
struct his own curriculum. Most of his energy was devoted
to opposing liberal theology, above all the "Higher Criticism" of scholars who sought to analyze the literary meth-
ods and sources of the biblical authors.

An incident occurred at this time that is worth noting,
because it illustrates Ronald Knox' deep commitment to
Anglo-Catholicism and his willingness to accept sacrifices
for religious principles. He had been hired to tutor Harold
Macmillan, the future prime minister, and a close bond of
friendship soon grew up between them. Knox shared with
Macmillan his enthusiasm about the Anglo-Catholic cause,
which met with the firm disapproval of Macmillan's family. At the end of October 1910, Ronald wrote to his sister
Winnie:

> "Could you rather pray for me? . . . I've a most heart-rending
> and nerve-racking dispute going on with Mrs. Macmillan, not
> about money this time, but about things 7000 times more im-
> portant. Don't tell anyone." In reply to Winnie's anxious en-
> quiry he explained that the family had asked him to give his
> word never to mention religion to Harold again. This Ronnie
> could not do, so he had to leave, and "by now I'm extremely
> (and not unreturnedly) fond of the boy, and it's been a horrid
> wrench to go without saying a word to him of what I wanted
> to say." [9]

Ronald Knox was ordained a priest of the Church of England on September 22, 1910; his father did not attend, unable to accept the rampant ritualism of the ceremony. The
youngest son of the Evangelical Bishop of Manchester had
thrown in his lot with the heirs of the Oxford Movement

[9] Fitzgerald, *Knox Brothers*, pp. 119–20.

and was intent on using his intellectual and rhetorical gifts to oppose the inroads of liberalism into Anglican theology.

At this point, when Father Knox was preparing to wage war on the Higher Critics, we should reconnoiter the complex ecclesiastical battleground he was entering. In spite of a powerful Evangelical awakening and the flourishing Anglo-Catholic revival of the Oxford Movement, the Church of England had inherited many problems from the nineteenth century. The Industrial Revolution and its consequent urbanization had disrupted the rural social structure of England, and with it the patterns of Church life. The Church was losing not only the working classes, but also the intelligentsia. Ecclesiastical control of education decreased, and leading figures in science and the humanities freely professed agnostic views. Developments in the critical study of history and literature called into question basic presuppositions of Christianity.

In 1889, Bishop Charles Gore and several other theologians published a response to this intellectual challenge, *Lux Mundi*. The contributors were primarily High Churchmen, and they sought to combine critical scholarship and orthodox faith. The nose of the camel of Higher Criticism was under the tent of Anglican theology. Yet, although the work was controversial, it did not create a major stir because its use of Higher Criticism was limited to the Old Testament.

It was when these same principles were applied to the Gospels at the beginning of the twentieth century that the storm broke. The Broad Church, allied to liberal Protestantism on the Continent, did not experience great difficulties with the use of Higher Criticism on Gospel texts: Jesus' moral teaching was of enduring value apart from the historicity of his miracles. The Low Church and Evangelical Free Church members were in a different situation. They could not accept such a challenge to the literal interpretation of Scripture and vigorously combatted it when it appeared in English theology.

The High Church presented a more complex picture. Especially after the Roman condemnation of Modernism in 1907, the pro-Roman element was suspicious of the Higher Criticism because it was seen as the fruit of liberal Protestantism. A second element of the High Church, represented by Gore and Edward Talbot, was favorable to Higher Criticism, but felt it was essential that its application be judiciously controlled. A third element, with such leaders as T. A. Lacey and William Spens, encouraged a more thoroughgoing application of its principles of interpretation; this group was influenced by George Tyrell, and thus in turn by Alfred Loisy and Albert Schweitzer.

The issue crystallized in 1910 with the publication in English of Schweitzer's *Quest of the Historical Jesus*. It was yet another attack on the literalist stance of the Low Church. But it also created problems for the Broad Church, since Schweitzer rejected the identification of the Kingdom preached by Jesus with the moral and social progress so central to liberal thought. And it was also a challenge to the moderate element in the High Church: if Jesus could be as mistaken about his fundamental understanding of the Kingdom of God as Schweitzer maintained, how could one put faith in his Gospel and his Person?

The problem took another twist a year later with the publication of *Miracles in the New Testament* by J. M. Thompson. Applying the principles of Higher Criticism, Thompson questioned the historicity of miracles, including Jesus' Virginal Conception and bodily Resurrection. This led to open warfare between those High Churchmen who favored a free application of the principles of Higher Criticism and those who felt it must be limited and controlled. As a clergyman of the Church of England, Thompson had to subscribe to the Articles of the Creed—which include Christ's Virginal Conception and bodily Resurrection. How, demanded Bishop Gore, could he do this and deny their historicity? The debate was public, bitter, and ironic: the very man who had sanctioned the use of the principles of Higher Criticism in 1889 opposed them in 1911. But it was not so much that Bishop Gore had changed; in fact, the whole situation had changed. In 1889, Gore had welcomed the Higher Criticism because it promised to reveal the historical foundations of Christianity. The sword had turned in his hand, and it now threatened to call these very foundations into question. Upon what basis, if not historical veracity, could Christians of the twentieth century establish their faith? Some, inspired by the work in the area of mysticism by Dean Inge, Evelyn Underhill, and Baron Von Hügel, responded, "religious experience". But Father Ronald Knox was definitely not of this school.

The tempest raised by Higher Criticism hit hardest at Oxford and Cambridge, at the very time that Ronald Knox was beginning his priestly ministry. He tried to enter into the minds of those who were attempting to see Christian doctrine in a new light, but it was no use. Even at Eton, Knox had been hostile to Higher Criticism—far more alarmed then at its implication for Homer than for the Bible (*SA*, 30)—and he remained antagonistic to it: "If I was to go to heaven with the Higher Critics, it must be on the plea that invincible ignorance blinded me to the light of doubt" (*SA*, 111).

Knox was disturbed by the doubts raised by Anglican Modernism; he was opposed to the form of literary criticism behind it. But many of its proponents were highly

respected scholars, and some were also his friends. How
could he oppose Modernism without appearing presumptu-
ous or disloyal? He used the weapon of humor.

He satirized Higher Criticism by employing its principles
to "prove" the multiple authorship of the Sherlock Holmes
stories and to suggest that the author of "In Memoriam"
was Queen Victoria.[10] He lampooned Modernism with a
limerick redolent with the language of the *Book of Common
Prayer*:

> O God, forasmuch as without Thee
> We are not enabled to doubt Thee,
>   Help us all by Thy grace
>   To convince the whole race
> It knows nothing whatever about Thee.[11]

But his cleverest attack came on the eve of the publication of
Foundations,[12] when he caricatured each of the contributors
in a pastiche of Dryden, entitled "Absolute and Abitofhell".
Here again he poked fun at the authorship theories of Higher
Criticism:

> Twelve prophets our unlearn'd forefathers knew,
> We are scarce satisfy'd with twenty-two:

[10] Ronald Knox, "Studies in the Literature of Sherlock Holmes", and "The
Authorship of 'In Memoriam'", in Ronald Knox, *Essays in Satire* (London:
Sheed and Ward, 1928).

[11] Ronald A. Knox, in *In Three Tongues*, ed. Laurence Eyres (London: Chapman and Hall, 1959), p. 123. This poem is titled "The Modernist's Prayer".

[12] *Foundations: A Statement of Christian Belief in Terms of Modern Thought*
(London: Macmillan, 1912) was authored by by "Seven Oxford Men"—
B. H. Streeter, R. Brook, W. H. Moberly, R. G. Parsons, A. E. J. Rawlinson,
N. S. Talbot, and W. Temple. According to the *Oxford Dictionary of the Christian Church*, "The book marked a definite stage in the current theological
debate and it experienced much immediate influence, but its optimistic liberalism and immanental standpoint proved increasingly unacceptable to suc-
ceeding decades."

A single Psalmist was enough for them,
Our List of Authors rivals A. & M.:
They were content Mark, Matthew, Luke and
    John
Should bless th'oldfashion'd Beds they lay upon:
But we, for ev'ry one of theirs, have two,
And trust the Watchfulness of blessed Q.[13]

He highlighted the prevailing mood of uncertainty that came
with Modernism:

When suave Politeness, temp'ring bigot Zeal
Corrected, "I believe," to "One does feel."[14]

Foundations not only provoked one of Knox' wittiest
satires, but also his first serious response to the challenge of
Modernist thinking: *Some Loose Stones*.[15] This work should
be considered in some detail, because the principles Knox
develops in it were to influence his religious outlook and
apologetics for the rest of his life.

In his opening chapter, he characterizes the contributors
to *Foundations* as religious leaders seeking to accommodate
religion to the man in the street; their operative question
—according to Knox—was "How much will Jones swal-
low?" But what people really want is not accommodation
but a clear statement of the beliefs of Christianity so they
can decide to accept it or some other religion,

[13] Ronald Knox, "Absolute and Abitofhell; or Noah's Ark put into Commission, and Set Adrift (with no Walls or Roof to Catch the Force of these
Dangerous Seas) on a New Voyage of Discovery; being a Satire in the Manner of Mr. John Dryden on a Newly-Issued Work Entitled *Foundations*", in
Essays in Satire, p. 87; reprinted in Eyres, *In Three Tongues*, p. 116.

[14] *Essays in Satire*, p. 85; Eyres, *In Three Tongues*, p. 115.

[15] Ronald Knox, *Some Loose Stones: Being a Consideration of Certain Tendencies in Modern Theology, Illustrated by Reference to the Book called "Foundations"*
(London: Longmans, Green, 1913); hereinafter, *SLS*.

It is in the second chapter that Knox develops his fundamental objection to the approach taken by the authors of *Foundations*: because Christianity is a revealed religion, the traditional theology of the Church begins with certain a priori principles and is deductive, whereas Modernist theology begins with hypotheses and is inductive. Knox maintains that this approach, rather than being more objective, alters and colors facts to serve the "tyranny of the hypothesis". Faith demands secure a priori foundations, and hypotheses by their very nature provide only a partial and uncertain representation of truth:

> This alone would give strong ground for doubting that the first principles of our faith were ever meant to rest on foundations so precarious. But it is not merely that they are insecure avenues to truth; my complaint is that they contain definite provocation to error. And on the ground of this constant temptation, of which I am myself fully conscious, if I could not preach the Christian faith in its fullness on a basis of absolute a priori certainty, I would give up preaching it altogether (*SLS,* 50–51).

Knox then takes up several individual theological issues raised in *Foundations* and critiques them in light of this inductive/deductive dichotomy. A few examples will illustrate his approach.

MIRACLES

In *Foundations*, these are reduced to special acts of Providence. But this robs them of their evidential value, and they were clearly evidential for the disciples of Jesus. If they were so clearly evidential, why did some disbelieve them? This ambiguity points to a need for a moral witness (Christ's teaching) to complement the witness of power. But the witness of power—for the disciples—cannot be dispensed with. For us, it is not reason but imagination that finds the miraculous difficult.

RESURRECTION

The modern prejudice against the miraculous leads to elaborate explanations for the empty tomb and the appearances of the risen Christ, whereas a bodily Resurrection—in a glorified state—is really the simplest explanation of the data. Our question should not be "Can we believe in the Resurrection in spite of such and such facts?" but "Knowing that Jesus rose from the dead, how can we explain such and such facts?"

INCARNATION

Traditional theology begins with the a priori idea that, if Jesus was God, he must have possessed the attributes of God: omnipotence, omniscience, impeccability; any limitations must be seen as a voluntary refusal to use these powers. Modern "Kenotic Theories" suggest that the Word was "undeified" in becoming man; thus, Christ was not divine in the sense of possessing divine attributes, but merely in the sense that his will was completely in accord with the Father's, and so divine in content. If that were true, then Christ's "divinity" differs from that of any other man only in degree, not in kind.

ATONEMENT

According to *Foundations*, Christ underwent "vicarious penitence" which was salvific because it revealed God's love and called mankind to conversion. For Knox, salvation entails more than moral transformation: sin has disrupted the whole created order and requires not only forgiveness but satisfaction. Only the suffering of the Sinless One, who is both God and Man, could compensate for the punishment deserved by our rebellion.

In the tenth chapter of *Some Loose Stones*, Knox leaves doctrine and considers the impact of the deductive and inductive approaches on practical religion. The two poles here are "authority" and "experience"; Knox is critical of reliance on experience because it cannot provide certainty.

He divides religious experience into three kinds. First, there are "abnormal", extraordinary revelations—visions, locutions, and so on. These have little evidential weight, because they are rare and difficult to evaluate as to origin. Secondly, there are inner psychic events—sudden conversions, feelings of intense devotion, an acute consciousness of God's presence; while these may help the recipient, they are transient and can disappear as inexplicably as they come. There is, thirdly, the routine inner life of any religious person. The problem here is that there is no guarantee of objective truth. How can we know if a religion is "right"? Appeal to the majority? But Christianity could be as false as the ancient Greek and Roman religions that had their day in the sun. Appeal to holy people? There are holy people outside Christianity. Finally, Knox points out that there is no such thing as a "pure" spiritual experience apart from authority:

> As a matter of modernist psychology, this appeal to experience is very interesting. The modernist will not allow himself to be regarded as in any way prejudiced in favour of one particular theological system. He therefore collects together the testimony of innumerable other people, primitive Bishops, medieval nuns, and contemporary charcoal-burners, who were and who are, beyond any shadow of dispute, prejudiced

theologians—prejudiced by what they believed upon a basis of purely traditional authority. And the result of this appeal is served up as if it were the most modern of all critical investigations, an essay in psychology. But if a priori assumptions are to play no part in modern theology, spiritual experience must play no part in modern theology, for spiritual experience is based on a priori assumptions (*SLS,* 193–94).

In his final chapter, "Jones at the Crossroads", Ronald Knox presents the dilemma of the contemporary believer: on one side lies the road of Modernism, on the other that of "complete intellectual suicide":

> He is looking nervously down each of these in turn; the one thing that never seems to occur to him is the thing which I want him to do, and that is to go straight on. Let him trust orthodox tradition to determine what he is to believe, *and common sense to determine what is orthodox tradition* (*SLS,* 216).

This seems to be an unsatisfactory conclusion. Ronald Knox has opposed experience to authority and demanded authority as the authentic basis for religious experience. The question still remains, "What authority?" To suggest that common sense determines what is orthodox tradition— could that not describe the project undertaken by the authors of *Foundations?* The basic thesis of *Some Loose Stones* is that a priori principles must take precedence over a posteriori evidence in revealed religion (*SLS,* 152). For the next several years, the great preoccupation for Knox was the search for the authority upon which all else could be built. It was not sufficient for this authority to be presumed; ironically, as Knox found, it had to be experienced.

2

CONVERSION
(1915–1926)

Father Knox invited his fellow Anglicans to abandon the winding, picturesque road of doubt and find in the Church's authority the straight, logical, businesslike road suited for pilgrimage:

> . . . straight, because it is the simplest way of accomplishing your journey; straight, because the whole business of faith is not picking and choosing your way, or looking out for sign-posts, but having the pertinacity to follow your nose; straight, because after all the road is very largely Roman (*SLS,* 217).

The question of authority was one which stirred considerable controversy in Anglican circles at the time. In 1914, the Bishop of East Africa permitted intercommunion between Anglicans and Nonconformists; a neighboring bishop had demanded that the Archbishop of Canterbury depose him for heresy. Some thought this "Kikiyu Incident" would cause Knox to "pope"; instead, he responded with another humorous poem, entitled "Reunion All Round", which ridiculed ecumenical indifferentism.[1]

In spite of his friends' fears that incidents such as this, or the conversion of the monks of Caldey Island, would

[1] Ronald Knox, "Reunion All Round", in his *Essays in Satire* (London: Sheed and Ward, 1928), p. 47.

send Ronald Knox into the Roman Church, he remained convinced that the authority he sought lay in the Church of England and that with time and study it would come to light.

Suddenly, there was no time. With the outbreak of the First World War, Knox' friends had to decide quickly whether or not to become Roman Catholics: the army made no provision for the theological distinctions between various Anglican "schools".

Ronald's closest friends, Harold Macmillan and Guy Lawrence, came to Knox and told him of their intention to go over to Rome, although in the event Macmillan remained an Anglican. According to Waugh,

> It was a day of revelation for Ronald, for he suddenly found that where his heart was most deeply committed, his ratiocinations were meaningless. There was nothing he could say, and nothing he wanted to say, to keep them at his side.[2]

The event was traumatic for Knox: he could ingeniously defend the Anglican Church, but he could not commend it to those he loved as they went off to face the prospect of death.

For the next two years, he endured a severe testing of his faith. He found himself questioning the validity of the Church of England, torn between despair at embracing any kind of supernatural religion and the thought of joining Rome—whose claims he had adroitly fended off for years. In 1916, he unexpectedly met the Jesuit C. C. Martindale at Lord Halifax' home and asked about being received into the Roman Catholic Church. When Martindale asked why, Knox said, "Because I don't believe the Church of England

[2] Evelyn Waugh, *Monsignor Ronald Knox* (Boston and Toronto: Little, Brown, 1959), p. 139.

has a leg to stand on." Martindale responded, "Why do you think that the RC Church has legs?"[3] Knox could not answer; he realized he had no positive reason for becoming a Roman Catholic.

He set about rereading Anglican works dealing with papal claims, such as Milman's *History of Latin Christianity* and Salmon's *Infallibility of the Church*. He no longer found their arguments against Rome persuasive. But he found another problem:

> For years my ten spies had told me that the promised land was impossible of entrance; how could I trust Joshua and Caleb when they had the same evidence at their disposal, and came back with the assurance that the promised land was mine? (*SA*, 196).

His father wrote to him concerning his attraction to Rome. In response Ronald employed an image hardly suited to dispel the apprehensions of the bishop:

> In reply Ronnie tried to explain his need for an absolute spiritual authority, comparing the Church of Rome to a shop-window in which there was no need to examine the goods, because over the door there was a sign THIS IS THE TRUE DEPOT ORDAINED BY CHRIST HIMSELF. "I should not have used the metaphor," the Bishop answered, yet he strove to understand.[4]

By the fall of 1917, Ronald Knox was completely worn out: the privations brought on by the war, the strained relations with his father, the anxiety concerning his friends at the front, and the two-year inner struggle regarding his

[3] Ibid., p. 146.
[4] Penelope Fitzgerald, *The Knox Brothers* (London: Macmillan, 1977), p. 140.

most cherished beliefs, had all taken their toll. He resolved
to go on retreat and come to a decision.

> My feeling was this. I had by now become so tired with my
> buffeting against the waves of difficulty that I hardly knew
> whether I believed in anything; whether I must not embrace
> my second alternative, and give up asserting supernatural re-
> ligion altogether. . . . Now, my retreat should be my *experi-
> mentum crucis*. If my acts (of resignation especially) during my
> retreat should result, as they well might, in revulsion from
> the whole thought of religion, then, for the time at least, I
> would own myself defeated. But if in the making of them
> I found that religion was still a real world to me, that my
> soul still functioned (after two years of vague aspiration and
> spiritual numbness) as a soul made to serve its Creator and
> to no other end, then it was all right. Then I would enter the
> Kingdom of Heaven as a little child; it was close to my hand
> (*SA,* 213–14).

He came to his decision, and on September 22, 1917, was
received into the Roman Catholic Church. Even in his relief
and happiness, Knox realized the pain his decision would
bring to others. He wrote to his sister Winnie:

> Just for yesterday, I allowed myself to be happy, because it *is*
> nice to have come to a determination, but between now and
> Saturday (when I'm to be received) I'll be having to write a
> very unhappy series of letters. Most of the time I've prayed
> in the chapel here, I've been kneeling under a statue of St
> Louis, who holds a crown of thorns. . . . It's so hard now to
> think of anybody but Paw. . . . It's so hideous to feel I'm not
> in the least worth all the trouble I'm causing.[5]

In order to appreciate the direction Ronald Knox' apologetics took after his conversion, it is necessary to consider

[5] Quoted in Waugh, *Monsignor Ronald Knox*, p. 159.

the position of the Catholic Church in England at the time he entered. Intellectually, the aftershocks of the Modernist condemnation were still being felt. Socially, the Catholic Church was becoming more accepted and was seeking increased "respectability", thanks to the growing number of talented converts who were eloquently stating her claims. The anti-Modernist position was enthusiastically embraced by Knox. Years later he recalled that he was more zealous in this regard than his new co-religionists:

> I came into the Church, it seems to me, in a white heat of orthodoxy, Manning's disciple more than Newman's; and when I took the anti-modernist oath, it was something of a disappointment that the Vicar-General was not there to witness the fervour I put into it—he had gone out to order tea (*SA,* xx).

The Catholic Church in England going into the twenties was seeking to create a parallel Establishment of aristocracy, public schools, and universities: "The trained intelligence of the Jesuits was directed to organizing a cricket match at Lord's which would be as smart as Eton and Harrow."[6] Ronald Knox was seen in this context as an ornament, complementing as a secular priest the efforts of the Benedictines, Jesuits, and Dominicans.

Finally, mention should be made of the Catholic literary revival in which Knox figured prominently. Almost all of these Catholic writers were converts, and their intertwined stories are related masterfully in Joseph Pearce's *Literary Converts*.[7] Throughout the twenties and thirties, their writings gave English Catholicism a high profile. Frank Sheed

---

[6] Fitzgerald, *Knox Brothers*, p. 176.

[7] Joseph Pearce, *Literary Converts: Spiritual Inspiration in an Age of Unbelief* (1999; San Francisco: Ignatius Press, 2000).

lists the following—in addition to Knox and Martindale
—as the principal contributors to English "convert liter-
ature": Christopher Dawson, E. I. Watkin, Alfred Noyes,
Roy Campbell, D. B. Wyndham Lewis, J. B. Morton, G. K.
Chesterton, Eric Gill, David Jones, Compton Mackenzie,
Philip Gibbs, Maurice Baring, Arnold Lunn, Sheila Kaye-
Smith, Bruce Marshall, Graham Greene, and Evelyn Waugh.[8]
Much of their work presented the case for Catholicism, ei-
ther directly or indirectly, and Ronald Knox was one of the
more brilliant stars in this firmament.

Knox generally shied away from controversy in his first
years as a Catholic, and although he wrote at times on religious issues, he avoided sectarian issues directly. One work
dealing with the subject of conversion is worthy of note:
Anglican Cobwebs.[9] In this book, he addressed, not the doctrinal difficulties, but the personal and emotional issues involved in leaving the Church of England. Here he reveals his
"affective" side, sympathetically exploring the spiritual and
interpersonal challenges that must be met when someone
considers changing religious affiliation.

Knox' popular writings in the twenties included two novels dealing with religious themes. *Other Eyes Than Ours*[10] is a
clever diatribe against Spiritualism, but apologetical themes
do not figure strongly in it. In the second, he is still grap-
pling with the problem of authority. Its title alone reflects a
certain ambiguity he felt: *Sanctions: A Frivolity*.[11] The plot involves a conversation among various guests at a house party
about such issues as the ideal person, the role of the state,

---

[8] Frank Sheed, *The Church and I* (New York: Doubleday, 1974), pp. 96–
97.

[9] Ronald Knox, *Anglican Cobwebs* (London: Sheed and Ward, 1928).

[10] Ronald Knox, *Other Eyes Than Ours* (London: Methuen, 1926).

[11] Ronald Knox, *Sanctions: A Frivolity* (London: Sheed and Ward, 1932).

and the task of education—the underlying question being, "What are our sanctions for deciding right and wrong?" The question had a deeper urgency for the disputants in the wake of the carnage of the First World War, which had revealed the demise of so many moral presuppositions and values in Europe. Picking up the pieces of these shattered illusions, the characters explore various possible foundations for belief and conduct: tradition, science, religious experience, progress, revelation. Knox leaves no doubt where his own sympathies lie, but the other positions are by no means "straw men", and when the party breaks up, there is only a hint that one of the characters has moved toward Catholicism.

This novel reflects the importance he still attached to authority. Its implications had broadened beyond the question of religion. As Knox noted elsewhere, the question of sanctions was basic to human nature:

> Hypnotized by his crowd sense, the [plain] man nods his head in solemn approval when Walt Whitman or Ella Wheeler Wilcox thunders against formulas and creeds; left to himself, with the consciousness that he is no longer applauding a scene but living out, behind a lowered curtain, the all-important drama of his own earthly existence, he can turn nowhere without awakening the echoes, *Is it true? Is it right?* Granted that he can always shelve merely speculative difficulties, he still cannot face life with its maddening complications, without facing also the insistent question, *What is my duty?* Nor can even the speculative difficulties remain indefinitely shelved; parenthood sees to that.[12]

---

[12] Ronald Knox, introduction to *God and the Supernatural: A Catholic Statement of the Christian Faith*, ed. Father Cuthbert (London: Longmans, Green, 1920), p. 8. Knox requested that this essay be omitted from the 1936 edition, as no longer giving an accurate picture of religious life in England.

3

CHAPLAINCY AT OXFORD
(1926–1939)

In 1926, Ronald Knox was appointed chaplain to the Catholic students at Oxford, a post he held until 1939. The appointment put him more in the public eye as he returned to the world where in his youth he had established his reputation as a wit and brilliant debater.

The announcement of Knox' appointment may have caused some discomfort at Oxford: the *enfant terrible* of the Anglo-Catholic movement was returning and would use his intellectual and oratorical gifts to entice a new generation into the Church of Rome. Such fears were groundless. Because of his shyness and his unwillingness to take advantage, Ronald Knox avoided convert work. He never accepted the title "Catholic Chaplain at Oxford" used by his predecessor, because he felt it implied an official status he did not have; he referred to himself as "Chaplain to the Catholic Students at Oxford". And he once remarked to Arnold Lunn, "The Church gets on by hook and by crook, the hook of the fisherman fishing for converts and the crook of the shepherd looking after his flock, and I am more of a crook than a hook."[1]

As shepherd to the Catholic students at Oxford, Knox

<hr>

[1] Arnold Lunn, "Ronald Knox: A Tribute", *Critic* (Oct. 1957): 9.

sought to establish contact with each individually and make himself available to them for counseling. Unfortunately, his reputation for brilliance and his diffidence created a gap between him and the students, and he regretted that they did not find him more "approachable". However, in his weekly conferences, he provided an important service to the undergraduates.

When permission was given for Catholics to attend Oxford, Cardinal Manning had stipulated that they had to receive ongoing instruction in their faith. It was the responsibility of the chaplain to provide this. Knox was well-suited for the task: he knew the kinds of questions the students were facing and the pressures they experienced. In his conferences, he responded to their difficulties with insight and imagination.

As can be seen from the outline Knox provides in "The Whole Art of Chaplaincraft", the structures of these conferences followed the traditional lines of Catholic apologetics:

> The first year is fairly simple; the autumn goes into the existence of God; the spring term to the revelation made by Our Lord; the summer term to the position of the Church as the organ of Revelation. In the second and third year I have tried courses on the four last things, on science and miracle, on the Mystical Body, on Faith, on the history of the Church or of the Holy See, on Science as it is sometimes represented in opposition to religion and so on. But always the ninth term has been devoted to a course on sex and marriage.[2]

According to Waugh, Knox "was not training apologists to speak in Hyde Park, but ordinary men living in the world, who should be able to give an account of their Faith when

---

[2] Quoted in Evelyn Waugh, *Monsignor Ronald Knox* (Boston and Toronto: Little, Brown, 1959), p. 230.

it was challenged in ordinary social intercourse".[3] Many of these conferences reached an audience beyond Oxford when they were published in 1942 under the title *In Soft Garments*.[4] In 1952, he published another set of his conferences on the same subjects given at Oxford in the years following his term as chaplain.[5]

In 1927, Ronald Knox made his contribution to a series of books on the theme "I Believe" with the publication of *The Belief of Catholics*.[6] It was his first effort to present a synthesis of Catholic faith for the general public and has remained one of his most popular books.

Knox begins his study with the modern distaste for religion: a general decline in church membership, religious commitment, and dogmatic teaching mark the twentieth century. Renewing a theme from *Some Loose Stones*, he maintains that people are not drawn by the accommodation of the churches: "Dogmas may fly out at the window but congregations do not come in at the door" (*BC,* 11).

Yet, as Knox notes, there is one body that in the first decades of the twentieth century has experienced continued growth in England, the Roman Catholic Church. Why? Knox considers several possible explanations: her ceremony, her history, her universality; but these are really "accidental" and not unique to Catholicism. The great attraction of the

[3] Ibid., p. 230.

[4] Ronald Knox, *In Soft Garments: A Collection of Oxford Conferences* (London: Burns and Oates, 1942); reprinted in *University Sermons of Ronald A. Knox, Together with Sermons Preached on Various Occasions*, ed. Philip Caraman (New York: Sheed and Ward, 1963); hereinafter *US*.

[5] Ronald Knox, *The Hidden Stream: A Further Collection of Oxford Conferences* (London: Burns and Oates, 1952); reprinted in *US*.

[6] Ronald Knox, *The Belief of Catholics* (London: Ernest Benn, 1927); references in this book are to the 4th ed. (London and New York: Sheed and Ward, 1953); hereinafter *BC*.

Church is her authority; the Catholic Church meets our human need for sanctions. For a variety of reasons, then, people are attracted to the "Shop Window" of Roman Catholicism, but they cannot bring themselves to enter the store because they fear that the price of admission is intellectual suicide. They cannot "open their mouth and shut their eyes" to accept everything on the authority of the Church.

This total reliance on the authority of the Church is a common impression of non-Catholics, and it is one Knox wishes to dispel. He states that the following basic Catholic doctrines are not accepted primarily on the basis of authority but on reason: the existence and nature of God; his revelation in Christ; the broad outlines of Christ's life, death, and Resurrection; his foundation of the Church; the teaching authority of the Church. He then treats each of these questions in turn.

Concerning the existence of God, Knox prefers to follow the avenue of establishing the reality of God from the evidence of creation. The existence of the idea of God in the mind does not necessarily prove his existence in fact, and "experiences" of God, while persuasive to the person who has them, have little evidential value to one outside the experience.

Moving from the God of creation to the God of revelation, Knox uses a clever technique to help his readers realize the amazing contents of the Bible, which familiarity with the stories tends to dull. (At this point in the argument, he does not attribute any inspired status to the Scriptures, since this is taken on the authority of the Church; he is considering them here as human documents, reliable in at least general outline as to history). He invites his reader to cover the text of the New Testament with his hand and consider the Old Testament in isolation. The ability of the Jews to retain their uniqueness in the midst of their neighbors is notable: their courageous tenacity in embracing monotheism, their fierce exclusivity, their absolute conviction that God is working in a special way in their history are an invitation to consider the possibility that God does act in history. And this activity has a strong future orientation; the events are interpreted by the Jews as promises of yet greater acts to come.

Next, Knox invites his reader to move ahead to the year 90, with his hand still over the New Testament, and look at the secular sources that speak about Christianity: it is seen as a force to be reckoned with, demanding the attention of civil administrators who aim at "breaking the butterfly sect upon the wheel of imperial efficiency" (*BC,* 73). The movement is widespread, organized, draws on all classes, and is centered on a cult of Christ. Nonbiblical Christian sources from the same period (such as the Letters of Ignatius and the Letter of Clement) confirm the basic characteristics reflected in the secular sources. They also underscore Christian self-identity in the face of both the pagan religions and of Judaism.

Knox invites his reader to move his hand and look at the Epistles in the New Testament. Here again, the uniqueness and universality of the Christian community are evident. On the basis of these letters alone, one would know a great deal about the faith of the early Christians, especially their belief in the Resurrection of Jesus.

So, looking ahead from the anticipatory flavor of the Old Testament, and looking back from the rapid emergence of a body of people distinct from the Jews and visible enough to attract the attention of the government in various parts of the Roman Empire, Knox directs his readers to the missing piece: the Person of Jesus. The reader is invited to uncover the Gospels and ask, "What claim did Jesus make?"

Did he claim to be God? Explicitly—Knox answers—no;

but his manner of referring to his relation with the Father, his unique claims to authority, his performance of signs and wonders in his own name all point to his implicit claim to divinity.

Knox offers three possible explanations for this claim: either Jesus was an impostor, or he was mad, or he was telling the truth. Was he a fraud? This is doubtful, since Jesus consistently rejected any of the benefits that would be the motive force behind the imposture. Was he insane? This is difficult to square with the insight, soundness, and beauty of his teaching; but it is the only sensible explanation—unless Jesus was right.

What is the evidence that might justify Jesus' claim? Knox suggests (1) the fulfillment of the Old Testament—not of specific texts but of the general expectation behind the prophetic literature; (2) the wisdom of Jesus' teaching; (3) his miracles; and (4) above all, his Resurrection. Concerning the last, Knox notes that Jesus expected to rise from the dead and that his tomb was in fact empty. The best natural explanation for this is that the disciples stole the body; but psychologically, it would have been difficult for this frightened group of followers to have staged such a deception and willingly embraced death for what they knew to be a fraud. Finally, they reported appearances of Jesus after his death. This evidence does not produce mathematical certainty, nor should it be expected to. Historical evidence can only be expected to remove reasonable doubt—and according to Knox, the Gospel records of Easter faith can do this.

The discussion now moves to the stumbling block between Catholics and Protestants, the nature of the Church. Christ left no writings; he did leave his example, but more importantly he left a community to continue his work. This was a visible community, composed of weak and strong alike, but one that could act and teach with the authority of Christ—otherwise, how could the revelation of Christ be prolonged with any kind of certainty? This living, visible body requires a visible focus of unity and a final arbiter in fundamental disagreements about the belief and conduct of the community; and the most likely candidate for this office would be the successor of the Apostle who held this position in the earliest Christian community, Saint Peter.

Up to this point, Knox has claimed that the matters under discussion are not believed by Catholics primarily on the basis of authority, but reason. His chain of argument has led to the assertion that the Christian community in union with the successor of Peter is guided by Christ and with his authority teaches infallibly. Once the inductive conviction of the infallibility of the Church is made, her doctrines follow deductively. These doctrines cannot originate in reason, because they are revealed by God and must be accepted on divine authority. Among these doctrines are the Trinity, creation and Fall of first parents, redemption, Incarnation, Virgin Birth, the Church as the Body of Christ, the sacramental system, the Real Presence of Christ in the Eucharist, the Last Things. For Catholics, these are not simply a series of statements. Rather, they are a manifestation of the supernatural life that is part of the air Catholics breathe: "Faith knows what it does not experience. It is a conviction, not a consciousness, that the other world is close at hand" (*BC*, 150).

For the remainder of *The Belief of Catholics*, Knox seeks to share something of Catholicism as it appears from the inside: her moral teaching, sacraments, ascetical theology, religious orders, saints, and understanding of non-Catholics. He concludes with a prediction that the great conflict of the future will be between Catholicism (for which the individual is the starting point) and secular social and humanitarian systems (for which the race as a whole is central): "Our work is to colonize heaven, theirs to breed for Utopia" (*BC,* 212). The course of events since Knox made that prediction have confirmed how right he was.

As was seen above, Father Knox limited his work at Oxford to those who were already Catholics. He did not seek out converts at Oxford or elsewhere, observing to Arnold Lunn, "as a rule no good is done by arguing the Catholic case with an individual unless he has already begun to be attracted by the Faith."[7] However, in his writings, his sermons, and his conferences, he did influence many people; and while Wilfred Sheed may be guilty of hyperbole when he claims that Ronald Knox created an intellectual fad of Catholicism at Oxford, it is true that "he made countless young intellectuals and sophisticates realize that there was nothing shameful about being a Catholic."[8]

Hilaire Belloc wanted to enlist Knox' talents in his crusade to reestablish Christendom, and as early as 1923 wrote to him:

> "*Être Catholique, c'est tout.*" To remake Europe is our intense and urgent call. Of the higher things I know nothing. I was not called to them. But I know *that*: and I know that very few men can so act anywhere: in England but a dozen, and that you are one of them.[9]

Knox was not to be his champion; he had slaked his thirst for "causes" in his Anglican days. He produced some controversial works in the early 1930s, but for the most part

[7] Arnold Lunn, "Ronald Knox: Some Memories", *The Month* (Nov. 1957): 269.

[8] Wilfred Sheed, "Monsignor Knox: A Reluctant Legend", *Catholic World* (Feb. 1957): 366.

[9] Quoted in Waugh, *Monsignor Ronald Knox*, pp. 200–201.

his influence was indirect and exercised through the bonds of friendship. Pearce's *Literary Converts* describes the elaborate network of relationships among English converts, and Ronald Knox had a part to play in the conversions of several important figures.

Knox and G. K. Chesterton were linked by ties of mutual admiration. On the occasion of Chesterton's death, Knox wrote to his widow:

> He has been my idol since I read the Napoleon of Notting Hill as a schoolboy. I'll only hope that you, who know as no one else does what we have lost, will find it easy to imagine as well as believe that he is alive and unchanged. Thank God for that faith; that I have it when so many friends lost it was due, I think, under God to him.[10]

For his part, Chesterton felt that Knox and Maurice Baring had done the most to help him decide to become a Catholic. In fact, in 1922, Chesterton wrote Knox to request convert instruction. Both men encountered scheduling difficulties, and finally Chesterton asked to receive instruction from Father John O'Connor, the inspiration for his fictional detective Father Brown. Upon hearing this, Knox wrote to Chesterton:

> I'm awfully glad to hear that you've sent for Father O'Connor and that you think he's likely to be available. I must say that, in the story, Father Brown's powers of neglecting his parish always seemed to me even more admirable than Dr. Watson's power of neglecting his practice; so I hope this trait was drawn from life.[11]

Ronald Knox preached at Chesterton's funeral. Chesterton had in earlier times offered to Knox the tribute of a poem:

[10] Quoted in ibid., pp. 197–98.
[11] Quoted in ibid., pp. 198–99.

> Mary of Holyrood may smile indeed,
> Knowing what grim historic shade it shocks
> To see wit, laughter and the Popish creed
> Cluster and sparkle in the name of Knox.[12]

The relationship between Ronald Knox and Arnold Lunn is especially interesting because, although Lunn could not strictly speaking be called Knox' convert, Knox did play a significant role in bringing Lunn into the Church, and their discussions were conducted publicly by means of a book they coauthored, *Difficulties*.[13] In the 1920s, Arnold Lunn was so irritated by the conversions of Knox, Chesterton, and others that he wrote a critical study of them, *Roman Converts*.[14] He sent a copy to Knox and was surprised to receive the following reply: "Thank you for the compliment, for it is I suppose a compliment of sorts, like the crocodile pursuing Captain Hook."[15] Years later Knox confessed to Lunn,

> You narrowly escaped receiving the most terrific snorter. I had just drafted it out. Instead, with a real effort, I sat down and wrote a reasonably polite reply. This would seem to be one of the few occasions on which doing the right thing has had the right results.[16]

[12] G. K. Chesterton, "Namesake", from *Collected Poems of G. K. Chesterton* (1927), quoted in ibid., p. 189. Reprinted by permission of A P Watt, Ltd. on behalf of the copyright holders, the Royal Literary Fund.

[13] Ronald Knox and Arnold Lunn, *Difficulties: Being a Correspondence about the Catholic Religion between Ronald Knox and Arnold Lunn* (London: Eyre and Spottiswoode, 1932). A second edition, with two additional letters, was published in 1952; references in this book are to the 2nd ed.; hereafter, *Dif.*

[14] Arnold Lunn, *Roman Converts* (London: Chapman and Hall, 1924).

[15] Lunn, "Knox: Some Memories", p. 263

[16] Ibid.

In 1930, Lunn suggested they team up and write a book discussing the problems of belief. Both men agreed that apologetical works where a believer presented both sides of the argument were unconvincing. *Difficulties* consists of a series of letters by Lunn setting out objections to Catholicism, with responses by Knox. The book is not systematic, and it ranges from questions concerning particular Catholic practices to serious philosophical obstacles to belief. Knox' replies are not always persuasive, which adds to the book's appeal: the argumentation in *The Belief of Catholics* appeared airtight, and there is perhaps an apologetic value in watching the believing opponent now and then scramble to return a serve.

In 1952, *Difficulties* was republished, with an additional letter from Lunn (now a Catholic) and Knox. Looking back on the correspondence, Knox wrote that its value lay not so much in the arguments presented but in the opportunity of "seeing a fellow creature snap-shotted in the act of getting the grace of faith", adding:

> It was a good thing, I think, that you did not choose a more adroit opponent; it might have looked as if you were being battered, by sheer force of reasoning, into submission. In proportion as the reader is led to exclaim, 'Fancy being convinced by arguments like that!' he will perhaps be led to wonder whether it is, after all, entirely a matter of argument. *Di me terrent, et Jupiter hostis*[17]—you were up against something you hadn't bargained for, and it wasn't me (*Dif*, 261).

[17] A quotation from Virgil's *Aeneid* 7.895. Turnus says to Aeneas, "Your threatening words do not frighten me; it is the gods I fear, and my enemy Jupiter."

In the early 1930s, Ronald Knox produced two other lengthy pieces of controversial writing. The first of these, *Caliban in Grub Street*,[18] was an attack on the "Symposiasts"[19] who felt free to discuss religious matters in a popular vein, although for the most part they had no theological training. Robert Speaight sums up Knox' book in this way:

> *Caliban in Grub Street* was an answer—agile, witty, and not in the least ill-tempered—to what may be described as popular modernism; to what modernism had become by the time the dons had done with it. In trying to rescue an ethical Christ from the Christ of "the Churches", the Symposiasts had reduced to nonsense the Gospels to which they made their highly selective appeal, and the early Christian history of which they knew nothing whatever. "I believe" had indeed degenerated into "one does feel."[20]

This book was followed two years later by a work in a similar vein, *Broadcast Minds*.[21] Here Knox' concern was with the great credence people put in anything they heard over the radio, and the danger that this was robbing them of discernment. (Knox had firsthand experience of such credulity: in 1926 he had broadcast a parody of a BBC newscast, describing an imaginary riot in London led by "the National Movement for Abolishing Theatre Queues"; it caused a near-panic.) "Broadcastmindedness" was the name he gave this temptation: "the habit of taking over, from self-constituted mentors, a ready-made, standardized philosophy of life, in-

[18] Ronald Knox, *Caliban in Grub Street* (London: Sheed and Ward, 1930).

[19] They range from Bertrand Russell to Rebecca West and include such figures as Arnold Bennett, H. G. Wells, and Hugh Walpole.

[20] Robert Speaight, *Ronald Knox the Writer*, published together with Thomas Corbishley, *Ronald Knox the Priest* (New York: Sheed and Ward, 1965), p. 198.

[21] Ronald Knox, *Broadcast Minds* (London: Sheed and Ward, 1932).

stead of constructing, with however imperfect materials, a philosophy of life for oneself".[22]

His immediate concern is the unquestioned authority of "Science", and the impact of pundits who have as their theme the antipathy between science and religion when they take to the airwaves. The core of the book is a critique of the "Omniscientists"[23] and their views on religion. The book concludes with a warning that science should not be allowed to usurp authority outside its own proper sphere:

> Science has an honourable mission, but it is not that of moulding the whole character of a civilization. It can show us the means to a given end . . . but it can tell us nothing about the value of the end proposed, and humanity, to the last, will remain free to decide what ends it thinks admirable. This, as a rule, scientists recognize. . . . But of these modern priests of science I am more doubtful; they mean business, and they talk the language of fanaticism.[24]

Difficulties was Knox' last purely controversial work. Perhaps, as Waugh suggests, "Ronald felt that in arming Sir Arnold and putting him in the field, he had fulfilled his own combatant duties."[25] Perhaps he felt that his books, though entertaining, were ineffectual:

> He had used the weapon of laughter in addressing himself to people who could no longer laugh, and the weapon of reason in talking to people who could no longer think and the weapon of knowledge in informing people who were indifferent to fact. And even if he had demolished the pundits, he

[22] Ibid., p. 10.
[23] These included Julian Huxley, H.L. Mencken, Gerald Heard, John Langdon-Davies, and H.G. Wells.
[24] Knox, *Broadcast Minds,* p. 275.
[25] Waugh, *Monsignor Ronald Knox,* p. 236.

had put nothing in their place. . . . Certainly, Ronald Knox, when he looked back on his years of controversy, was well aware that he had not pierced the sound barrier.[26]

And so, after thirteen years as chaplain, Knox resolved to leave Oxford.

[26] Speaight, *Ronald Knox the Writer*, p. 203.

4

THE WAR YEARS
(1939–1945)

Two years before leaving Oxford, Father Knox was asked to give instruction to Lady Daphne Acton. Although he did not as a rule give convert instructions, he did take on the task when asked by personal friends. Lady Acton had already read a great deal about Catholicism before she began formal instruction and proved to be both a good pupil and a frank critic of Knox. More than that, she gave him the gift of deep friendship. A letter written by Evelyn Waugh to Hubert Van Zeller in 1957 suggests that her influence on Knox affected his apologetics:

> More than once Daphne refers to your opinion (if you it was) that she was a good influence on Ronnie in making him 'less intellectual'. Could you give me some light on your meaning? Did you simply mean that in a human, social way he was in danger of becoming donnish, or was their [sic] a spiritual sense in which his Faith was too much a matter of reason and that she helped to give it life?[1]

It is certain that she chided Ronald Knox for wasting his talents (while on a cruise she threw his latest—and last—

[1] Mark Amory and Michael Davies, *The Letters of Evelyn Waugh* (London: Weidenfield and Nicholson, 1977), p. 495.

detective story overboard), and she encouraged him to use his gifts more creatively. The immediate results were one of Knox' finest novels, *Let Dons Delight*[2] (dedicated to her), and his resolve to pursue the possibility of producing a new English translation of the Bible.

The "nine years hard" Knox devoted to his translation of the Vulgate Bible occupy a central place in his biographies. In light of subsequent Catholic biblical scholarship, it seems as much a "period piece" today as the *Spiritual Aeneid*; but it played a significant role in preparing people for the later English translations. It was also, in the opinion of Christopher Hollis, not only a work of scholarship but an essay in apologetics; an intelligible translation of the Bible would be of great help to English people.[3]

More specifically, to English Catholics. Coming from an Evangelical background, Knox was both amazed and troubled by Catholic ignorance of the Bible. He hoped above all to produce a translation that would help Catholics develop the habit of using the Bible in their personal prayer. On this score, among the laity, Knox encountered "bleak indifference, varied now and again by . . . puzzled hostility",[4] and his fellow priests were not much more exemplary:

> The clergy, no doubt, search the Scriptures more eagerly. And yet, when I used to go round preaching a good deal, and would ask the P.P. for a Bible to verify my text from, there was generally an ominous pause of twenty minutes or so before he returned, banging the leaves of the sacred volume

[2] Ronald Knox, *Let Dons Delight: Being Variations on a Theme in an Oxford Common Room* (London: Sheed and Ward, 1939).

[3] Christopher Hollis, "Review of *Monsignor Ronald Knox* by Evelyn Waugh", *Critic* (Feb.–Mar. 1960): 32–33.

[4] Ronald Knox, *Trials of a Translator* (New York: Sheed and Ward, 1949), p. 72.

and visibly blowing on the top. The new wine of the gospel, you felt, was kept in strangely cobwebby bottles.[5]

To wipe the cobwebs off the bottle, Knox retired to the Actons' house at Aldenham and devoted himself to the task of producing a readable translation of the Bible.

Unfortunately for Knox the translator, but fortunately for Knox the priest and apologist, he soon had company. At the outbreak of the Second World War, Assumption Convent in Kensington Square was evacuated to the Actons' estate. One can imagine Knox' jaw dropping as he watched his sanctuary invaded by a pack of schoolgirls and all his translation apparatus crowded into one small room.

So once again Ronald Knox was a chaplain, but no longer in the familiar world of Oxford. His charges were not sophisticated college students, but children. They were also girls; Knox had discouraged female students to come around the chaplaincy at Oxford. And they were not a flock he had been sent to tend; they were an intrusion visited upon a middle-aged scholar, which threatened to take time away from his assigned task of translating the Bible.

What promised to be a most unpleasant situation turned out to be one of the greatest blessings of his life. He found the girls very easy to get on with—their youthfulness allowed their affection to overcome their awe. He established abiding friendships with several of them and, in the years following the war, was often called upon to preside or preach at their weddings. Furthermore, they continued the process begun by Daphne Acton: they helped Ronald Knox overcome his orientation toward the past and to recognize his stake in the present and in the future.

They also challenged Knox to present the Catholic faith

---

[5] Ibid. P.P. designates the pastor of a parish.

to a new audience, young people. Many of these conferences were published after the war: *The Creed in Slow Motion*,[6] *The Mass in Slow Motion*,[7] and *The Gospel in Slow Motion*.[8] They proved to be among Knox' most popular books. The organization and arguments employed are similar to those of the Oxford conferences. What is of value in these conferences is, not his argumentation, but his imagery and language. They show Knox at his most imaginative and playful.

Here are a few examples:

[Speaking of the struggle between life and death in nature:] It's like a perpetual deuce-game in tennis; vantage-in every May, and vantage-out every November (*CSM,* 119).

The shepherd doesn't run after his sheep when they get straying; he shouts to his sheep-dog, and the dog runs after them, barking at them in a very rude way. When you see a sheep-dog doing that, it ought to remind you of my sermons . . . (*CSM,* 61).

If you can imagine Princess, harnessed the wrong way round in a pony-cart, so as to face it, being pulled by the pony-cart down a very steep hill—that is the sort of thing that is happening to us all the time since the Fall (*CSM,* 69).

"What is truth?" Pilate asked, and it serves him right that he should be put there in the middle of the *Credo,* as if the Church were determined to go on saying to him, to the end of time, "Here, you fool, this is!" (*CSM,* 82).

The same man who could write a pastiche of Dryden or capture the flavor of English spoken in Common Rooms

[6] Ronald Knox, *The Creed in Slow Motion* (New York: Sheed and Ward, 1949), hereinafter, *CSM.*

[7] Ronald Knox, *The Mass in Slow Motion* (New York: Sheed and Ward, 1948).

[8] Ronald Knox, *The Gospel in Slow Motion* (New York: Sheed and Ward, 1950).

over three centuries met the challenge to present the Catholic faith in the language and images familiar to a schoolgirl.

Father Knox shared the privations and uncertainties of the war with these unexpected guests, and continued his work on the Bible. On August 6, 1945, his world changed with the dropping of the atomic bomb on Hiroshima. He was horrified at its use and wrote a letter to the *Times* pleading for the Allies not to use such a weapon again. The letter was not mailed, because when Knox was on his way to post it, he heard that the Japanese had surrendered. But for Knox, the problem raised by the bomb did not disappear with the conclusion of the war. "Hiroshima" meant not only the destruction of a city—it meant the destruction of a world view, and it was important for him to work out its implications. Customarily a careful writer who could spend months polishing a single chapter, Knox was galvanized into activity, and in only two months created one of his most remarkable essays, *God and the Atom.*[9]

In his reflection on the significance of Hiroshima, Knox employs a psychological structure: trauma, analysis, adjustment, sublimation. The trauma has struck at the ordinary person's sense of cosmic discipline—an order inherent in nature, an optimism in human progress, and the validity of our moral judgments: "The shadow of that airman [flying to Hiroshima] will then strike him with a faint, simultaneous chill of doubt, of despair, and of guilt" (*GA*, 11–12). Knox then analyzes this threefold trauma.

The first chill, doubt, strikes at faith. Knox, who had sought to demonstrate evidence for God from order in creation, considers the implications of the idea that a kind of anarchy seems to reign in the heart of nature. He compares

[9] Ronald Knox, *God and the Atom* (New York: Sheed and Ward, 1945), hereinafter, *GA*.

three "worlds" that give very different testimony about "reality": common sense ("the very solidity of the object in front of us acts as a kind of fulcrum against which the agility of the intellect can brace itself", *GA,* 37); metaphysics ("all docketed and labelled like an album with pressed flowers in it", *GA,* 37); and physics ("rotating, coruscating, ebullient with paradox", *GA,* 37–38). Atomic physics calls into question the most basic ideas not only of metaphysics but of common sense.

The second chill, despair, threatens hope. Hope here is connected with a belief in Providence, which in the popular mind has been identified with three successive centers over the past one hundred years: first the individual, then the destiny of the nation, finally world progress. This last stronghold has been breached by the bomb, which has deepened the twentieth century's sense of doom.

The third chill, guilt, threatens love. Knox does not dwell on the morality of the bombing of Hiroshima, although he says it would have been a more perfect thing not to have done it. His concern is rather for present feelings and future implications. The war has conditioned people to violence. And at a time when self-restraint is so essential, there is instead a prejudice toward self-assertion: the fact that the bomb was used will weaken the voice of self-restraint and of charity.

In the next part, "Adjustment", Knox offers an alternative to these conditions. The unpredictability of an atom's explosion seems to replace the dogma of order in nature with pure chance: "It is as if we woke up one morning to find plums growing on the apple-tree" (*GA,* 105). Yet there *is* order in nature, and this "indeterminacy" at the heart of it only makes the mystery more profound—and an awareness of this can bring us to marvel again at the power of the

Creator: "We had admired the pattern as a mosaic; admire it more, now we find its medium to be a powdery gesso which, nonetheless, does not slip between the Craftman's fingers" (*GA*, 110).

In offering an alternative to despair, Ronald Knox compares the changing moods of Western civilization with the individual's growth in the spiritual life. Up to the First World War, Europe—especially England—was buoyant with a sense of progress and achievement; from 1914, there was a feeling of helplessness and discouragement. These alternating periods of presumption and despair are mirrored in the individual's ascent to God: moments of intimacy followed by "dark nights" where the best one may be capable of is behaving as if he had hope. Mankind is being called to exercise this virtue of hope, and Christians have a special responsibility not to abandon others by adopting an otherworldly attitude: "We should do better, I think, to help man the pumps of the labouring ship, and let the world see that hoping is one of our specialties" (*GA*, 128).

The third alternative Knox offers in the Adjustment section is what he calls "an alternative to decadence". Although atomic energy has been used to blast things apart, its primary function in nature is to hold things together; thus it may well serve as a symbol of integration. This *should* be the work of religion, which is all too often reduced to living according to a code. Rather, religion should simultaneously convey love for a person, loyalty to a cause, and conviction about a system of thought—which are the binding forces of an integrated person.

In a concluding chapter, entitled "Sublimation", Knox pleads for a wise use of atomic energy. Its discovery has been a gift of God—and all God's gifts are terrible, because along with them he has given us free will, "a wand that turns everything to meat or poison for us" (*GA,* 158). Whether this new energy will be used to make or mar the world—on a scale formerly undreamed of—will depend on man's wisdom and man's holiness. Knox' final plea is for saints:

> For the Saint, whose life supremely realizes the integration I have been trying to describe in this chapter, is, like the atom, incalculable in his moment; holds, like the atom, strange forces hidden under a mask of littleness; affects the world around him, as atomic energy does, not in an arithmetical but in a geometrical ratio—his is a snowball influence (*GA,* 166).

God and the Atom was one of Knox' most important books; it was also one of his least successful. It came too soon. As Waugh notes, "It was a moral and philosophical tract offered to a public obsessed by practical politics. . . . He felt himself charged with an urgent message of consolation to a people who did not know that they had been hurt."[10]

5

FINAL YEARS
(1945–1957)

After the war the Actons emigrated to Rhodesia, and Knox was invited to live with friends at the Manor House, Mells, in Somerset. Here he completed his translation of the Bible and devoted himself to other literary endeavors.

The questions raised by Hiroshima about so many of his presuppositions caused Knox to reexamine the views he had so tenaciously held. In his preface to the 1950 edition of the *Spiritual Aeneid*, he observed:

> Our tastes change insensibly. . . . Even over our most consid-
> ered judgements, part (we thought) of the very stuff of our
> minds, a haze of uncertainty has crept. Are we as convinced as
> ever that psycho-analysis (or, it may be, post-impressionism)
> is all mere nonsense? . . . An uneasy suspicion haunts us that
> you could, without self-contradiction, maintain the contrary
> (*SA,* xii).

He felt that his years as a Catholic had mellowed him, and he was not left high and dry when "the tide of literalism has receded, and the attitude of the Catholic authorities toward the findings of modern scholarship, though it is still one of caution, is no longer one of anxious suspicion" (*SA,* xx).

This warmth of human sympathy is to be found, for example, in his introduction to a series of letters published as *Off the Record*. The letters are his responses to inquiries for the most part on intellectual questions about the Church. But Knox introduces them by writing:

> Here, under a mask of anonymity, you have a glimpse of thirty or forty human souls that asked advice from a stranger. How many others are there, too shy, too proud, too dilatory to invoke any human counsellor in their bewilderment? We jostle them day by day without knowing it; joke with them, weary them, perhaps dis-edify them. Something is lacking in our prayers if we forget the secret maladies of men's hearts.[1]

One book from these final years should be singled out: *Enthusiasm*, which was Knox' own favorite of all his writings, and one that had occupied him for over thirty years. Its roots are to be found in the chapter of *Some Loose Stones* dealing with authority and experience. Begun shortly after his conversion, the book was intended as a historical survey of the chaos that results when (Roman) authority is rejected and experience becomes the touchstone of religious truth. But that was not the book Knox ended up writing, as he admitted in his introduction:

> All my historical figures, Wesley himself included, were to be a kind of rogues' gallery, an awful warning against illuminism. But somehow, in the writing, my whole treatment of the subject became different; the more you got to know the men, the more human did they become, for better or worse; you were more concerned to find out why they thought as they did than to prove it was wrong.[2]

---

[1] Ronald Knox, *Off the Record* (New York: Sheed and Ward, 1954), p. x, hereinafter *OR*.

[2] Ronald Knox, *Enthusiasm: A Chapter in the History of Religion, with Special Reference to the XVII and XVIII Centuries* (Oxford: Clarendon Press, 1950), pp. v–vi.

It is interesting to note that Knox concludes his book by pointing out that the history of religious enthusiasm contains a cautionary warning to the Catholic Church:

> Where wealth abounds, it is easy to mistake shadow for substance; the fires of spirituality may burn low, and we go on unconscious, dazzled by the glare of tinsel suns. How nearly we thought we could do without St. Francis, without St. Ignatius! Men will not live without vision; that moral we do well to carry away with us from contemplating, in so many strange forms, the records of the visionaries. If we are content with the humdrum, the second-best, the hand-over-hand, it will not be forgiven us.[3]

How much Knox' views had changed can be seen when considering his final apologetical work, *Proving God: A New Apologetic.*[4] Knox had conceived the idea of a new approach to apologetics in 1955 and made an attempt to begin the book, but then put it aside to translate the autobiography of Saint Thérèse of Lisieux. What little he had written of the former was published posthumously by Evelyn Waugh. Knox begins by contrasting youth with old age; in fact, though he does not say so, *his* youth with *his* old age. Young men see visions; they discover an idea that gives them a clue to the riddle of life. Everything *must* be seen in the light of this idea: "If it is to retain its spell over him, it must at all costs be coherent; he is less concerned to discover whether it corresponds with the facts of the world outside" (*PGNA,* 9). But with old age can come tolerance, the ability to see value in another's point of view. "The world is no longer divided into angels who agree and devils who disagree with

[3] Ibid., pp. 590–91.
[4] Ronald Knox, *Proving God: A New Apologetic,* with a Preface by Evelyn Waugh (London: *The Month,* 1959), hereinafter, *PGNA.*

him. . . . Experience has softened the hard edges of his affirmations. If I may use words in a grossly unphilosophical sense, what he demands now is not so much truth as reality" (*PGNA*, 10).[5]

The subject of this "old man's book" is the Christian revelation. There is a shadow of the young Knox: revelation comes from God; its assertions cannot be verified by reference to experimental knowledge: "If you live to be ninety, the doctrine of the Trinity is no more provable or probable to you than it was when you were nineteen" (*PGNA*, 10). But here is the shift: revelation comes from God to people, and so must be presented in human language and terms:

> Thus the presentation of the divine fact to the human mind calls for persuasion; and if you would persuade, you must have some knowledge of how people's minds work, of the ideals which move them and the prejudices which enchain them. Experience is no longer to be despised, and even an old man's book may be worth the writing (*PGNA*, 11).

Because of this change in perspective, Ronald Knox now sees much of Catholic apologetics (presumably including his own) as "inhuman"—its mathematical precision affects the contemporary person with a feeling of *malaise*: "our answers seem too glib, too 'slick'; there is something machine-made about them" (*PGNA*, 12).

Knox finds the root of this dissonance in history. Since the Enlightenment, Reason has been unduly exalted: "like

[5] In a previously unpublished conference, Knox contrasts Catholic and Protestant apologetics: "I would say that the Protestant approach to apologetics gives the ordinary Englishman an impression of reality without truth, while the Catholic approach to apologetics gives him an impression of truth without reality." "Humanizing the Third Proof" (conference, 1943). Text may now be found in Milton Walsh, *Ronald Knox as Apologist* (S.T.D. diss. Gregorian University, Rome, 1985), pp. 307–30.

fire, it is a good servant but a bad master" (PGNA 13). And now, by reaction, we are in an age of "unreason": in Germany, Lutherans are turning from rationalism to Pietism; in France, "Existentialism has threatened, by a kind of palace revolution, to dethrone the intellect" (*PGNA,* 14); while in England, the solemn doubts of the Victorians are not challenged—they are simply written off as bad form.

Should Catholicism haul down the flag of intellectualism? No, but perhaps it has been too inclined to isolate it from moral and spiritual witness. We Catholics, Knox points out, are so fond of the word "instruction":

> A recent convert, say, has made a wrong marriage; we fall back
> on the comment, 'He must have been very badly instructed.'
> As if nobody ever sinned except for want of information!
> Or do we, perhaps, imply that the convert was taught what
> Christ's law is, but not taught to love it? (*PGNA,* 16).

Ronald Knox temporarily set aside *Proving God* to translate the autobiography of Saint Thérèse of Lisieux. His father had still been vigorous at eighty, and Knox felt he had many years ahead of him. So did others. Frank Sheed recalls thinking that, whereas most of Knox' spiritual writing had been wholly intellectual, "that time seems to have ended. There is a meditation on Our Lady in *A Retreat for Priests* which promises writing of great spiritual depth still to come. After all, he is only sixty-eight."[6]

A year later Knox was dead. He was taken by cancer of the liver, which was fatal within months. At the time of his death, Ronald Knox was eulogized for his preaching, literary style, and humility. The impression that emerges from these obituaries is that he was a persuasive apologist above all because he spoke and wrote of what he had made his own,

---

[6] Frank Sheed, *The Church and I* (New York: Doubleday, 1974), p. 120.

and because, in spite of his remarkable gifts, he considered himself ordinary and attempted in his preaching and writing to address the ordinary person's concerns. In his panegyric, Martin D'Arcy summed up in a few words Ronald Knox the apologist:

> If we look back at the long list of his writings, we see that they have no other interest than to support either the natural or the supernatural order of God's creation. He did not attempt to invent something new; he did not try to keep up with the latest fashions in philosophy, art or literature, and he used his Dryden-like power of satire to ridicule the pretentious, the mystagogic and the sophistical. He had a deceptive simplicity, never pressing for novelty, but bringing out from God's treasures what was both new and old and so clothing it with words that it struck the mind with an unforgettable truth.[7]

[7] Martin D'Arcy, "Panegyric for Right Reverend Monsignor Ronald A. Knox", *Tablet* (Aug. 31, 1957): 172.

PART TWO

FINDING THE TREASURE:
THE ACT OF FAITH

6

AQUINAS OR PASCAL?

Introduction

How do we come to believe? In his writings and conferences, Ronald Knox did not strive to break new ground but
to present a reasoned argumentation for what we might call
"mere Catholicism" as attractively as he could. In later life,
he became increasingly dissatisfied with the "inhuman atmosphere" surrounding nearly all Catholic apologetics (*PGNA,*
11). His discontent is significant, because it strikes at the
very core of his purpose: Should the apologist aim for the
head or for the heart? As a theoretical question, this issue is
explicitly addressed in *Proving God*:

> Man is called upon to serve God with his whole heart and his
> whole mind, not with a fifty-fifty amalgam of the two. The
> two faculties should, by rights, function together as smoothly
> as the two lobes of the brain. In practice, they have to be stimu-
> lated alternatively—and by a single process, because the recog-
> nition of our own inadequacy as creatures is at once the guar-
> antee of God's existence and the basis of all worship (*PGNA,*
> 43).

To present the case for religion in this integral way is no
easy task: it will be necessary to combine "the lucidity of
St. Thomas with the unction of Pascal" (*PGNA,* 43).

Adumbrations of this theoretical problem may be found
in some of Knox' other writings. In his later Oxford conferences, for example, he raises the question, "Does Proof

Matter?" (*US*, 159–65), and he recognizes that the "apologetic man", who starts by believing in nothing and at the end of three years emerges as a convinced Catholic, doesn't really exist at all (*US*, 251). He shares with these students his awareness that "Few things are so disappointing in life as the experience, gradually borne in upon one, that it is very difficult to convince people by the arguments which seem satisfactory to oneself" (*US*, 256).

His most explicit statement of the tension between "reasons of the mind" and "reasons of the heart" is found in an introductory preface written by Knox for the English translation of Jean Mesnard's *Pascal: His Life and Works*.[1] Contemplating the "dazzling fragments of that tessellated pavement which Pascal never lived to finish", his *Pensées*, Knox says,

> And behind it all lies the doubt whether he was attempting the impossible, or whether he was solving at a blow the age-long difficulty of apologetics, when he set out to convince man's mind and man's heart at a single stroke, instead of appealing first to the one and then to the other. Would the finished work have been a rival to the *Summa contra Gentiles*, or a rival to the *Exercises*? Or would it, miraculously, have been a rival to both?[2]

Knox' own speculation on apologetics is also unfinished. In *Proving God*, we encounter an old man doubting not the sureness of his aim but the nature of his target. What role do the head and the heart play in coming to believe?

---

[1] Jean Mesnard, *Pascal: His Life and Works*, tr. G. S. Fraser, with a preface by Ronald Knox (London: Harvill Press, 1952). The preface may also be found in Ronald Knox, *Literary Distractions* (London and New York: Sheed and Ward, 1958), pp. 78–82.

[2] Knox, *Literary Distractions*, p. 82.

The Intellect

When Ronald Knox zealously swore the "Oath Against Modernism", he professed the teaching of the First Vatican Council that faith is not "a blind sense of religion welling up from the hidden depths of the subconscious under the impulse of the heart and a morally trained will, but a real assent of the intellect to truth received by hearing from an external source."[3] For many reasons, Catholic theology in the first half of the twentieth century continued to train the spotlight on the intellect when considering the act of faith. Knox was in sympathy with this emphasis. In his apologetical writings, he attempted to demonstrate the intellectual appeal of the Catholic faith. Accordingly, as the role played by the intellect enjoyed pride of place both for Catholic theology and for Knox, it is appropriate to begin with it when looking at the act of faith as presented in Knox' writings.

The intellect is essential both for coming to faith and for explaining faith. Faith must be founded on an intellectual conviction, such as, for example, that Christ is divine. While not every Catholic can be expected to lecture on the intellectual foundations of the faith, every Catholic should be able to give a reasonable account of his faith. Reason is the bridge between believer and unbeliever.[4] Knox exhorts his Catholic hearers to avoid using the teaching authority of the Church as an excuse for not giving an intellectual justification for their belief: "That is running away from your Cross."[5]

[3] The Oath against Modernism, Denzinger-Schönmetzer, 3542.

[4] Ronald Knox, *The Occasional Sermons of Ronald Knox*, ed. Philip Caraman (London: Burns and Oates, 1960), p. 356, hereinafter OS.

[5] Ronald Knox, *Pastoral Sermons of Ronald A. Knox*, ed. Philip Caraman (New York: Sheed and Ward, 1960), p. 376, hereinafter PS.

Knox presumes the general reliability of the intellect, and he argues that an unprejudiced examination of the motives of credibility presented in Catholic apologetics can so satisfy the intellect that the inquirer is brought to the point of making an act of faith (*BC,* 36).

The Catholic case for faith is based on evidence, but Knox is careful to point out that we should not expect such evidence to produce mathematical certitude. As one of his characters says in *Sanctions,* "The Gospel has to depend on human evidence, and what human evidence is there that can't be doubted?"[6] The most that can be hoped for is a "moral certitude", a human conviction that excludes reasonable doubt. How much evidence is needed to reach such a conviction? Knox recognizes that this is a subjective matter:

> Commonly the sceptic averts his mind from the Resurrection as I avert mine from the flying saucers. Where, exactly, the dividing line comes in between high probability and nonmathematical certainty is an uncommonly ticklish point.[7]

In a letter to his friend Laurence Eyres, he states that this "non-mathematical certainty" is all that should be sought:

> But there is, in judgements of facts, a more and a less degree about the certitude with which one holds them. E.g., I could, by consulting parish registers etc., acquire more certitude than I have at present that I am the child of my reputed parents, but the certitude I hold at present is so strong as to exclude all reasonable doubt, and that's all that's needed for a human action. The mistake is to suppose that, having such a conviction as that as to the truth of the Gospels, the

[6] Ronald Knox, *Sanctions: A Frivolity* (London: Sheed and Ward, 1932), p. 217.

[7] Knox to Mr. Davies, Feb. 9 [no year given], Knox Papers, Mells, Somerset.

meaning of our Lord's words, and so on, it should still be necessary to wait for an extraordinary flood of illumination on the top of that before making one's submission. That may be vouchsafed to some, but it is certainly not vouchsafed to most people: they have to proceed, in taking the step, on a strong human conviction, and it's only in the taking of it that it becomes the strongest certitude of their lives.[8]

Faith itself is a gift of God, and its impact so far as the intellect is concerned is to transform the nature of the believer's certitude: "The water of conviction is changed into the wine of faith" (*BC,* 145). In line with the teaching of the First Vatican Council, Knox conceived of faith as believing something to be true on the authority of God. Because the One in whom we put our faith can neither deceive nor be deceived, the divine gift of faith makes our certitude *absolute.*

In one of his Oxford conferences, Knox expands on this idea and makes some important distinctions.[9] There are, he says, three kinds of certitude: logical, psychological, and theological. Concerning logical certitude, the act of faith makes no change: the convert cannot produce more or better arguments than he could have given before coming to faith. Psychological certitude ("My dear chap, it absolutely bowled me over", *US,* 256) *may* accompany the act of faith; but again, it may not, and in any case it will probably not be permanent. It is the presence of theological certitude that is decisive; this transforms reasoned certitude and elevates it to a supernatural plane. Since grace does not necessarily move on the conscious level, the recipient of this gift may

[8] Ronald Knox to Laurence Eyres, July 18, 1920; in "Letters from R. A. Knox to L. E. Eyres", ed. L. E. Eyres, typescript, University of London, p. 44.
[9] Ronald Knox, "The Act of Faith", in *US* 251–57.

not always be aware of its presence. Knox finds evidence of this gift in his own experience only with the passing of years: so many certitudes of youth—about writers, artists, even religion and the values of life—do not seem in later years as absolute as they once did; but faith remains "an inalienable part of your make-up; not something which you have got hold of, but something which has got hold of you" (*US,* 257).

However, if faith does not alter logical certitude, neither can it eliminate the role of reason. The act of faith does not involve a "leap in the dark" that goes against the intellect; rather, reason is followed to its legitimate conclusion (*BC,* 146). Knox emphasizes this point when contrasting the ordinary Christian and the "enthusiast":

> If I may be allowed the use of a crude and inexact analogy, I would say that the human mind, upon accepting the Christian revelation in the ordinary way, becomes a constitutional monarchy. The speculative intellect, which till now reigned arbitrarily, still rules, but hedged about with custom and precedent; its range is limited by something other than itself. . . . In the mind of the ordinary believing Christian, the two principles of reason and revelation are interlocked; a theologian will sort them out and delimit their spheres for you, but in everyday life there is an unconscious give-and-take which regulates your thought without friction. It is not so with the convert to enthusiasm. In his mind, a sudden *coup d'etat* has dethroned the speculative intellect altogether; it remains a mere puppet monarch, signing every paper that is given to it with a rubber stamp.[10]

What is the kingdom ruled by the intellect, albeit constitutionally, after conversion? Knox calls it "mystery":

[10] Ronald Knox, *Enthusiasm* (Oxford: Clarendon Press, 1950), p. 586.

Faith is the first duty of the Christian, and mystery is the food of faith. . . . You admit, not grudgingly but with pride, that there are truths in the world too deep for your limited human understanding, and you salute them reverently as something out of your reach (*US*, 263–64).

The mysteries of the Christian faith are not like the mysteries in a detective story that baffle our guessing powers. They seem more than improbable, they seem impossible. In one Oxford conference, Knox examines several of these mysteries, noting that "If you gave a rapid sketch of Christian doctrine to somebody who was quite new at it, and asked, 'Come, isn't that reasonable?' you wouldn't get very far" (*US*, 259).

The mysteries he considers are the Trinity, the Incarnation, the Real Presence of Christ in the Eucharist, and free will. In each of these doctrines, the problem is that one can see two sides of the truth, be certain both of them are true, and still not see where they dovetail into one another. Yet these are not simply religious mysteries; they are human mysteries. They occupy "a kind of no-man's land between the incredible and the understandable".[11] Free will is not simply inexplicable in relation to grace; it is mysterious in itself and has engendered philosophical speculation even outside Christianity for centuries. The relationship between a thing in itself and the impressions it makes on our senses is not a puzzle only in regard to the Eucharist. It is not only the incomprehensibility of God that makes reflection on the Trinity or the Incarnation challenging; the very meaning of "personality", divine or human, is a riddle. Knox tells his audience:

[11] Ronald Knox, "What I Believe", in *What I Believe: Broadcast Talks*, ed. A. D. Ritchie et al. (London: Porcupine Press, 1948), p. 35.

You may picture human thought as a piece of solid rock, but with a crevice in it just here and there—the places, I mean, where we think and think and it just doesn't add up. And the Christian mysteries are like tufts of blossoms which seem to grow in those particular crevices, there and nowhere else (*US*, 260).

In a letter printed in *Off the Record*, Knox offers his own practical solution to such speculative problems:

My approach, which may seem to you a cowardly and perhaps even a dishonest one, is to stick firmly to that end of the mystery which seems to me lucidly obvious, and tell the other end of the mystery that it has jolly well got to square with that somehow. E.g. with grace and free will, being naturally a Pelagian, I say to myself, "I am certain of free will; and whatever the doctrine of grace means or doesn't mean, it must certainly fit in with this certainty of mine, and if I get to heaven I shall see how it does. Meanwhile I have got to accept it in blurred outline, and try to remember that there are other people whose difficulty is to believe in free will" (*OR*, 163–64).

The Will

Although Knox emphasizes the rational element in belief, it should not be presumed that he considers the act of faith to be the conclusion of a syllogism. In a spiritual notebook, he wrote: "I have kept the faith, in spite of all people had to say in defence of it."[12] The Catholic faith is not only a doctrinal system. It is also a life, a warfare, a loyalty, and a romance (*PS*, 184). Christianity addresses not only the mind but also the heart; it engages the will and the affections (*PS*, 153). Speaking of Newman's conversion, Knox says that revealed

[12] "Sayings of Mgr R. A. Knox", *The Month* (Aug. 1959): 109.

truth does not merely claim the homage of the intellect, it satisfies the aspirations of the heart:

> What Newman gained in 1845 was not the mere saving of his own intellectual honesty; it was a system of spiritual values which lit up the world for him; not a cold glare but a warm blaze, a kindly Light which made the darkness more congenial than the garish day he loved once (*OS*, 250).

This "kindly Light" responds to a deeply felt, human longing for something outside ourselves, which gives us the strength to keep on going, a loyalty and a direction that help people "to save themselves from the alternative of committing suicide or collecting postage stamps" (*US*, 72). According to Knox, this "something" can take three forms: it may be a personality, or a cause, or a philosophy. The Christian faith embraces all three. Membership in the Church identifies us with a movement, commits us to a system of beliefs, and above all takes us out of ourselves by demanding that we throw our reliance on a personality—the personality of Jesus Christ (*US*, 72–73).

This longing gives a much-needed urgency to the intellectual exploration of the Christian faith. In regard to the act of faith, it is this longing that activates the will to make a judgment on the evidence brought before the intellect. It is possible to consider the case for Christianity, find the arguments consistent and flawless, and yet to withhold assent; to say, with Thomas, "I *will* not believe" (*US*, 144). This may be due to a positive prejudice, but more often it is caused by the inclination against affirming anything when it is much simpler to take refuge in saying, "Yes, I suppose so." What Knox is talking about is in effect the difference between notional and real assent:

> There is all the difference in the world, practically, between saying, "Yes, I suppose that is true," and saying, "By Gad,

that's true!" And the difference between the two attitudes arises, really, not out of the strength of the evidence before us, but out of our willingness to identify ourselves with the judgement which reason ratifies (*US*, 75).

It is the will that plays a crucial role in making this kind of assent; "intellect by itself never gets a move on" (*US*, 254). Faith must engage not only the mind but the whole person. Knox tells the schoolgirls at Aldenham that to believe means much more than merely not denying; it means caring desperately whether something is true or not:

> Put it this way. If somebody says to you, "Of course, your own country's rule in the Colonies is every bit as brutal as German rule in Poland," you don't reply, "Oh, really? I dare say it is." You care furiously about a statement like that. You may not have the facts at your fingers' ends, but you are not going to let a statement like that pass without examination (*CSM*, 6).

Intellectual arguments for the faith, important as they are, must not be mistaken for the totality of the faith. It is not enough for the mind to consider "motives of credibility"; the will must come into play so that a judgment is made. It is this decision that makes the difference between notional and real assent.

Grace

Although we touched upon it briefly in our treatment of the role of the intellect, the supernatural aspect of faith calls for explicit consideration. Actually, Knox has little to say concerning the role of grace in the act of faith. This reticence can be understood if we recall that he is not interested in producing a systematic theological exposition on faith; he is interested in describing it from the human point of view. His starting point is more psychological than theological.

Still, his own experience and his deep spiritual life gave him a lively sense of the power of God's grace, and he reflected on how that grace interacts with our mind and heart:

> Considered as an intellectual process, it [faith] is inferior to reason, because it gives us no better than a dim and reflected light. But if you consider it as a gift infused by God, it is something higher than reason, because it breathes the air of a supernatural world which lies beyond all our experience. Your lamp may be brighter than the uncertain glimmerings of dawn; but those glimmerings are the foretaste, the reflected brightness of the daylight which is to come. So faith, less luminous to our minds than reason, is the foretaste of that fuller knowledge which we shall enjoy, please God in heaven (*PS,* 328).

Grace does not bypass the intellect or the will; the divine gift of faith elevates these human faculties.

Since faith is a gift, it can be withdrawn. The absence of the supernatural element is experienced on the human level. Grace will not override the natural faculties and maintain faith where there is no human cooperation.

Knox speaks of two ways in which faith can be lost, and they are connected to the intellect and the will. The first is a piecemeal process, in which intellectual conclusions are altered until they are no longer in harmony with Christian faith. The other, and probably more common way, touches on the will:

> You seem to lose all at once that faculty of affirming truth, of making its assertions your own, which we have seen to be involved in the nature of faith. It is not exactly that the motives for believing in God's existence, or of our Lord's Divinity, or the church's infallibility, look any different to you now as

compared with the way they looked yesterday; no, the whole thing looks probable enough, if you force yourself to face the issue, but it does not grip you, does not mean anything to you—your will has altered, not your intellect. You still hold the truth in your hand, but you no longer grasp it (*US,* 76).

Knox urges his listeners, university students, not to conclude from such an experience that they are necessarily losing their faith; it may be that they are simply losing the credulity of childhood. In any event, they should not abandon prayer, the sacraments, or the intellectual investigation of their religion. If they remain true to God, the obscurity will not be permanent (*US,* 77).

7

THE BRIDGE OF IMAGINATION

The old man setting out to find a new approach to apologetics felt that Catholic efforts tended to rely too heavily on intellectual argumentation. But what other common ground could there be between believer and nonbeliever? There seemed to be only one bridge, the bridge of reason. But another bridge did exist, one which John Henry Newman had described in the most significant nineteenth-century treatise on the nature of the belief, *The Grammar of Assent.*

The distinction between "notional" and "real" assent, so central in Newman's thought, was originally posed by him as a contrast between "notional" and "imaginative" assent. For Newman, a belief is only accepted when it is credible to the imagination. The act of faith emerges from a complex of historical, social, and reflective conditions; it is the fruit not of a conceptual demonstration but of a convergence of influences that reach us through our imagination.

Newman's theological method was grounded not only in philosophical analysis but in the literary affinities of the Oxford Movement, which reflected the influence of Joseph Butler and Samuel Taylor Coleridge. The Oxford Movement not only represented the theological program of Romanticism in England, but it also retained (at least up to the time of Newman's conversion) a sense of unity between literary culture and theological expression. The roots of this alliance between religion and imagination, of a "common grammar" for literature and theology, may be found in the Metaphysical Poets and Caroline divines of the seventeenth century.

Ronald Knox was familiar with Newman's *Grammar of Assent.* More significantly, he was shaped in his formative years by the structures and forces that preserved and fostered the common grammar between theology and literature: an education in the classics and Fathers of the Church, a love for the Metaphysical Poets, an interest in the Oxford Movement and the Gothic revival. It is not surprising, then, that in his counterattack to the inroads of Higher Criticism in Anglican theology, the young Father Knox pleaded with his fellow clergymen, "More dogma is wanted, pulpitfuls of it", and added, "your failure is a failure of imagination; you believe the doctrine, but you do not realize it" (*SLS,* 218).

Earlier in the same book, he considered the place of the imagination when treating of miracles. These, he maintained, are more a challenge to our imagination than to our reason. He explicitly noted the vital relationship between imagination and religion:

> "Imagination" is not necessarily the forming of ideas in the mind which correspond to nothing in fact. It is a quality necessary to the appreciation of truth. . . . Above all this faculty is necessary in Religion. I once heard a man in a public-house discussing the immortality of the soul; and he argued, oddly enough, that he could imagine living, say, several thousand years after bodily death, but he could not imagine living to all eternity. Of course we cannot fully imagine it; nor can we imagine infinite space, because we are so accustomed to finite space and finite periods. Nor do we find it easy to "imagine" miracles: we can accept them intellectually, and picture them

visually . . . but imagination still shies at them, and always will, though meditation may do something to bring it up to the fence (*SLS,* 66–67).

Later, as a Catholic, Knox noted that imagination travels in a world of space and sense and will not be satisfied with the answers that simply commend themselves to the reason (*PS,* 218). To appeal to the imagination, the apologist must leave the abstract for the concrete. Only in this way can belief move beyond the notional and inform all of life:

> We, in this tight-rope-walk business of trying to live our lives as if it really mattered, want more than a metaphysical conviction that God exists, want more than an ethical prejudice in favour of right-doing. Our fundamental beliefs, however incontestable they are on paper, have somehow got to be reduced to the scale of actual living, have somehow got to be interwoven with the fabric of our flesh-and-blood experience; we must be able to say, "It happened *then*"; we must be able to say, "It happened just *here*". We are creatures of dust, and a memory strikes down the roots of us more easily than a syllogism (*US,* 190).

Through his skillful use of images, Knox wove fundamental Christian beliefs into the fabric of our flesh-and-blood experience.

8

RONALD KNOX' USE OF IMAGES

Words are not coins, dead things whose value can be mathematically computed. You cannot quote an exact English equivalent for a French word, as you might quote an exact English equivalent for a French coin. Words are living things, full of shades of meaning, full of associations; and, what is more, they are apt to change their significance from one generation to the next. The translator who understands his job feels, constantly, like Alice in Wonderland trying to play croquet with flamingoes for mallets and hedge-hogs for balls; words are forever eluding his grasp.[1]

From a lifetime of playing croquet in the elusive world of language, Knox emerged as one of the most polished apologists for Catholic Christianity in the first half of the twentieth century. He was a master of prose, not its servant. In the words of Robert Speaight, some people wear their writing style like a fancy waistcoat; Knox wore his like a glove—it fitted exactly what he was saying.[2] His attention to the power and nuance of language serves to remind us that the *manner* and the *matter* of apologetics should never be separated.

---

[1] Ronald Knox, *Trials of a Translator* (New York: Sheed and Ward, 1949), p. 13.

[2] Robert Speaight, *Ronald Knox the Writer* (New York: Sheed and Ward, 1965), p. 101.

Metaphor

Ronald Knox knew that philosophy is suspicious of metaphor—"our symbols must go through a rigorous customs examination before they are chalk-marked as possessed of meaning"[3]—but he also recognized that they are essential to religious discourse: "I don't suppose you or I ever say a prayer without using a metaphor" (*US,* 175).

One of the jottings in his notebook suggests an important function of metaphor: "Most of us, at times, find a door which opens on the supernatural; the job is to get your foot into it."[4] Metaphor is that foot in the door, helping us to understand the mysteries of the Christian religion in terms of our human experience. Of course, even as he uses earthly metaphors to illustrate spiritual realities, Knox admits their inadequacy—with a simile: "It is like playing Wagner on a tooth-comb" (*PS,* 470).

Nourished on the metaphorical language of the Bible, Knox does not hesitate to draw on well-known scriptural images, stripping them of the tameness which accompanies familiarity. For example, most of us are as mediocre in our sin as we are in our virtue, and the forceful imagery of the Old Testament can appear to overshoot the mark, until Knox aims it in our direction: " 'Though your sins be of scarlet,' Isaias says, 'they shall be white as snow'—yes, that is splendid; but what is ever going to rid us of this prevailing tinge of pink?"[5] Even the most comforting of New Testament pictures is presented in a challenging way: "somebody ought

---

[3] Ronald Knox, *Lightning Meditations* (New York: Sheed and Ward, 1959), p. 129.

[4] "Sayings of Mgr R. A. Knox", *The Month* (Aug. 1959): 108.

[5] Ronald Knox, *Retreat for Beginners* (New York: Sheed and Ward, 1960), p. 93.

to paint a picture of the good Shepherd coming to rescue his sheep, and the sheep trying to get away" (*CSM, 62*). Knox' metaphorical "foot in the door" on the supernatural is a very human one. A favorite device is to interject an idiomatic expression or concrete image from daily life when speaking of spiritual matters. Concerning Paul's conversion he observes, "he came on board the Ark of Christ like a sailor who has been shanghied in the slums of a sea-port" (*OS, 389*). In the middle of a conference on God as Creator, he tells his schoolgirls, "I'm not here to answer the question, Why did God make ear-wigs?" (*CSM, 34*) Speculating on the afterlife, he notes that Virgil's heroes spend eternity looking after their horses and asks: "Do we, children of a later age, look forward to an eternity spent in washing down the car?" (*PS, 471*). Reflecting on the relation between religion and morality, he says that Christ "turned away from self-satisfied virtue, with its indefinable scent of floor-polish".[6] Such common and (certainly in the case of the earwig) garden variety images serve an important purpose. Their very particularity and "littleness" at first surprise, intruding into a refined discourse on the Creed; but upon reflection, this surprise brings home the lesson and reminds us that the mysteries of Christianity touch upon our ordinary daily lives.

Epigram

At times, Knox emphasizes the paradoxical aspects of Christian faith with the "shock tactics of an epigram".[7] In this he

[6] Knox, *Lightning Meditations*, p. 41.

[7] Ronald Knox, *Literary Distractions* (London and New York: Sheed and Ward, 1958), p. 63.

follows a literary tradition going back to Samuel Johnson, Richard Crashaw, and, more remotely, Ovid, Tacitus, and Martial. Paradox, for a Christian thinker, is not a far-fetched intellectual exercise:

> After all, if the thing is true; if God did lie in a stable, if the Eternal did die on a Cross, the paradox is there, hitting you in the eye. . . . Or again, if you live in a fallen world with a fallen nature, perpetually in love with a moral ideal which you find yourself incapable of achieving, it does not need a Crashaw to find paradox in the situation.[8]

These epigrams find a place in his conferences and in the monthly short sermons he wrote for *The Sunday Times*.[9] Here are some examples:

> Each of us must sink to child-level before the Crib; each of us, at the same time, must rise to the Incarnation-level (*CSM*, 4).

> It is only when we forget the dead that they are absent; we have but to kneel down, and they are present.[10]

> The magician tries to see how much he can get out of God for man; the priest tries to see how much he can get out of man for God (*US*, 154).

> We have seen his star, and our sympathies must be no narrower than his Planet.[11]

In some of Crashaw's poetry, Knox detects "symptoms of that over-subtlety, that straining after paradox, which was Crashaw's danger".[12] Mindful of this, he is sparing in his

---

[8] Ibid., p. 65.

[9] Two collections of these sermons were subsequently published as *Lightning Meditations*, cited above, and *Stimuli* (New York: Sheed and Ward, 1951).

[10] Knox, *Lightning Meditations*, p. 94.

[11] Knox, *Stimuli*, p. 22.

[12] Knox, *Literary Distractions*, p. 67.

own use of the epigram; in the words of Speaight, he is "constantly on guard against his own cleverness".[13] His intention is to instruct, not to impress. If he can enshrine a facet of Christian wisdom in a memorable phrase, fine; but an epigram should be a spice to enhance this wisdom, not a gravy to smother it.

Images of Place

Places exercised a powerful influence over Ronald Knox, as his *Spiritual Aeneid* testifies. He frequently uses the evocation of locale to draw his listeners into what he is saying. Philip Caraman notes how in his occasional sermons Knox surprised congregations with his precise knowledge of the history and topography of their parish or countryside (*OS,* vi).

Knox also realizes that the deep attachment to a city, and even to a particular street in a city, is a profoundly human emotion. Christ felt it when he contemplated Jerusalem:

> You see, he loved the city. Loved it with that divine love which his Incarnation mirrored on earth; "the Lord loveth the gates of Sion more than all the tabernacles of Jacob". Loved it, too, with a human love . . . he must have known what it was to love places, because of the memories which they enshrined and the traditions which they preserved (*OS,* 201).

Similarly, the Upper Room must have been a cherished site for the disciples:

> A room haunted with memories—through that door did Judas slink out into the night, so short a time since; on that

---

[13] Speaight, *Ronald Knox the Writer,* p. 103.

table the consecrated chalice reposed; through that window they listened to the shouts of "crucify him"; that floor had been trodden by impassible feet. It was in these surroundings that the Holy Ghost visited his people on the day of Pentecost. . . . The scene of their inspiration for the future was to be a scene enriched by past experiences (*PS,* 411).

Sometimes he uses modern locations to bring home a biblical story. For example, commenting on the parable of the derelicts invited to the wedding feast, he says, "It is the Embankment turned loose at the Guildhall" (*PS,* 313). Such local references have the advantage of involving his listeners in what he is saying; the disadvantage is that their particularity may limit their effectiveness for the reader. If one is unfamiliar with London, the words "Embankment" and "Guildhall" are meaningless. For this reason, Knox is circumspect in his references to specific locales.

Much more frequently he uses images of "place" in a broader sense: scenes from nature that are part of a wider human experience. Contrasts in nature—between night and day, winter and spring—are especially apt for illustrating the ambiguities and paradoxes of Christian faith. The perpetual tug-of-war between life and death in the seasons can be seen as an image of the struggle between sin and grace. But grace is stronger, for it is rooted in the garden of the Resurrection, which is "the nursery garden of the whole Church": "There is no autumn in your soul; as long as you believe in Jesus Christ and in what his Resurrection has done for you, it is always spring" (*CSM,* 123).

Jesus triumphs over both the autumn that follows him and the winter that precedes him. By the time of his coming, the glorious days of the Davidic dynasty were but a dim memory, the root of Jesse seemed condemned to eternal barrenness:

Yes, the old trunk, gnarled and withered, no more life in it now. And yet it is from that trunk that a single, slender branch is to come forth, a woman named Mary, of the house and lineage of David. She, in her virgin innocence, is to dare a man's winter with the promise of God's spring; she, by the miracle of her spotless motherhood, is to bear the one blossom that is to redeem our barren creation, and make it burst into flower (*PS*, 477).

A night traveler straining for the lights of home illustrates the searching gaze of the prophets; the same traveler leaving a lighted room and slowly coming to recognize objects around him on a moonless night depicts the Church in her centuries of reflection on the mystery of Christ.[14] And he points out for the benefit of those who attribute the attractiveness of the Church to "the sunset splendours of its decline" that they have only mistaken "the morning mists for the chill of sunset. Look about you; it is the dawn" (*US*, 360, 361).

One of his most imaginative "borderline" images is found in *A Retreat for Lay People*, in a conference entitled "The Spirit of Faith". He wishes to describe "that sheath of simultaneous attraction and repulsion which surrounds the Church".[15] This is faith, not as defined in the theological manuals but as encountered in real life: a quality that some people continue to possess, though they have given up any active participation in the life of the Church, and that others lack, though everything in their lives is directing them to the Church. Knox likens it to a wall of glass:

[14] Ronald Knox, "The Teaching Church", conference, n.d., Knox Papers, Mells, Somerset. Text may be found in Milton Walsh, *Ronald Knox as Apologist* (S.T.D. diss., Gregorian University, Rome, 1985), pp. 409–20.

[15] Ronald Knox, *A Retreat for Lay People* (London and New York, Sheed and Ward, 1954), p. 68.

> We will think of the windowpane as it shows on some evening
> of early autumn, when you have not the heart to draw the
> curtains on the lingering afterglow of sunset, yet have to con-
> fess that you cannot get on any longer without switching on
> the electric light. The effect of that upon insect life is curi-
> ous. . . . The ones inside, the ones you want to swat, are all
> making for the daylight; the ones outside, which you find
> yourself trying to swat by mistake now and again, are making
> for the glow of your electric lamp! And for the hundredth
> time you reflect, how odd it must be to be an insect, and not
> understand about glass.[16]

It takes a creative apologist to see a mosquito or a moth not
simply as an annoyance but as a parable on the nature of
faith.

The secret of this creativity is really no secret at all; Knox
shares it in his earliest theological book, *Some Loose Stones*.
In charging his fellow priests with a want of imagination, he
calls upon them to develop this faculty, not by reading hand-
books about dogma ("in which the latest honorary canon
triumphs over the latest German critic") but through meditation and prayer (*SLS*, 218). The images from nature Knox
uses to express Christian faith are the fruit of contemplation, not merely cleverness.

A question that surfaces from time to time in his writing
is, do you normally pray with your eyes shut or with your
eyes open? In spite of his contention that his generation
was formed in the first way and was not likely to change
(*GA*, 112), it is evident from his writings that Knox was
no stranger to either approach. His apologetics are rich in
imagery because in his own life he was able to approach
God through his creation, to catch a glimpse of him out of
the corner of his eye when contemplating the surrounding

[16] Ibid., p. 67.

world. In one conference, Knox suggests that where most books of meditation say, "Put yourself in the presence of God", he would like to change the formula: "Put yourself in the presence of something else, and find God there." Once again, there is the telling image:

> If you go out into the garden on a bright, sunny day, you don't look up at the sun and exclaim, "How beautiful the sun is!" You look round you at the flowers, at the dew on the grass, at the tree just in bud over there on the hillside, and exclaim, "How beautiful everything looks in the sun!"[17]

Images of Time

The theme of time is one that colors much of Knox' writing; with his gift for description and narrative, he uses history both to instruct and to entertain. He can throw the time machine into reverse and accurately re-create the conversation in an Oxford common room at fifty-year intervals back to 1588, as he does in *Let Dons Delight*. He can just as deftly put the indicator on "forward" and compose, in 1923, reminiscences from 1988 entitled *Memories of the Future*.[18]

Knox uses this facility with history to introduce his listeners into the events of salvation history. He invites them to imagine they are standing and looking into the tomb of the dead Jesus just before the stone is rolled across the entrance; and then to imagine themselves in the Upper Room with the disciples two days later (*OS,* 15). He asks them to

[17] Ronald Knox, *The Layman and His Conscience: A Retreat* (New York: Sheed and Ward, 1961), p. 49.

[18] Ronald Knox, *Memories of the Future: Being the Memoirs of the Years 1915–1972 Written in the Year of Grace 1988 by Opal, Lady Porstock* (London: Methuen, 1923).

identify themselves with the blind Bartimaeus, singled out for special attention by the Lord: "He's asking for you."[19] In one retreat conference, he even leads his hearers through the drama of Calvary, not as it would have appeared to one of the disciples or onlookers, but as it might have been seen by Jesus himself.[20]

Just as he can carry us back to biblical times, so he can bring the events of the Bible forward to help us understand later Christian insights. In a sermon on the Immaculate Conception, Knox uses the figure of Rahab to illustrate the Church's understanding of the role played by Mary in God's plan for redemption:

> One woman secretly held aloof from our conspiracy, secretly broke our covenant and kept herself pure from all spot; and through her our Jesus found a lodgement within the revolted city, conquered us and spared us and saved us from ourselves, through her. One traitress, by a noble treason to the sinful compact of her race, offered freely the only human help God deigned to use when he came to recover the allegiance of his rebels (*US,* 322).

Knox is serious but not solemn in his use of history. At times he can be whimsical in his effort to make the past come alive. In a sermon on Gregory the Great, he invites the schoolboys at Saint Edmund's to imagine themselves as slaves in the marketplace of ancient Rome:

> We think of the slave-boys looking very good and clean, like those cherubs with red cheeks and tow-colored hair on the Christmas cards. I daresay really English boys, even then, would have looked rather grubby little brutes, and no one would have mistaken them for Angels (*OS,* 21).

[19] Knox, *Layman and His Conscience*, p. 3.
[20] Knox, *Retreat for Lay People*, pp. 123–32.

The same imaginative power that lands English schoolboys
in sixth-century Rome can bring Thomas More into the
twentieth century:

> You can imagine him arguing over Plato with Dean Inge,
> or constructing imaginary worlds in collaboration with Mr
> H. G. Wells, or answering jest with jest, irony with irony, in
> a conversation with Mr Bernard Shaw (*OS,* 118).

Images of Childhood

Knox conjures up memories in his use of images from childhood. At times, he uses these images because he is talking
to children, as when he compares the reaction of a saint being forced to accept a bishopric to the tantrum of a child
being forced to take medicine (*OS,* 31). Speaking with children, he uses such images because he wants to draw on their
present experience. In his talks to adults, the images serve a
different purpose, one which he points out in a Christmas
sermon: "Christmas is a return to our origins. We make a
holiday of it, only if we have the strength of mind to creep
up the nursery stairs again, and pretend that we never came
down them" (*PS,* 354). He is inviting us to reenter the
world of childhood in which our imaginations functioned
more freely. And yet, in a sense, Knox does not bring his
listeners back; he addresses them as adults, whose horizons
are in some ways much broader than those of childhood.
Here is the foot in the door to the supernatural again: the
continuity/discontinuity of childhood and maturity offers
a good analogy to the relation between the natural and the
supernatural.

For example, he invites us to consider what happens when
someone gives a small child a gift. The child gazes at the

toy but never looks up into the eyes of the person who gave it. The mother has to extract some expression of gratitude from her child, while she really has to do the thanking herself. Knox then asks: "If we could see the Holy Eucharist at work, as the angels see it, I wonder if that isn't the light in which we should see our gratitude, and Christ's?" (*PS,* 224) The point is not the deficiency of our thanksgiving but that our experience is a thin slice of a reality beyond our possibility to comprehend now.

The vocabulary of Christianity freely applies parental images to God, to express his protecting and nourishing love. One of the things a parent does with children is to play games with them. Knox suggests that the whole drama of our relationship with God may be seen as a game:

> A child's games with its father, all the skill and foresight on the one side, all the romance and excitement on the other! . . . A father plays shop with his children, he with his own income, they with nothing but the pocket-money he allows them; and what complicated transactions take place, in make-believe! And so it is with the game of hide-and-seek, that goes on all through the centuries, that goes on in every man's life from the cradle to the grave (*PS,* 359).

Another childhood game offers a chilling image to illustrate the condition of those who die at the end of a life from which they have consciously excluded God: "It's as if a person playing blind-man's buff had suddenly torn off the bandage, only to realize that he was blind."[21]

It is a paradox, but Knox suggests that the best way for us to understand something of the life to come is for us to look at our past, to find in the continuity and discontinuity of our lives an image of the continuity and discontinuity

[21] Knox, *Retreat for Lay People,* p. 59.

between this world and the world to come. Our guesses may be feeble, but they are still valuable:

> You still find them childish, these analogies by which we try to realize the world beyond? Well, we are only children, all of us, hoping to grow up one day into the stature of the perfect man in Jesus Christ. And perhaps, if we are found worthy to do that, we shall see that these guesses of childhood were not altogether misleading; we shall smile at them, but we shall not disown them (*PS,* 474).

9

EXPERIENCE, REASON,
AND AUTHORITY

Knox holds in theory that reason is the common ground for believer and unbeliever, and so his formal approach to apologetics is strongly intellectual. As a matter of practice, he finds his meeting place to be the world of ordinary human experience. Of course, this does not exclude either the intellectual or formally religious aspects of human life: following the logic of a clear argument can be very satisfying, and most (if not all) people have had "numinous" experiences of some kind. The advantage of drawing on ordinary experience is twofold. First, it is universal: it appeals to what is common to all people, not just those with a philosophical or mystical bent. Secondly, it is immediate: the listener does not hear something he will have to think about; the image from daily life evokes an unreflected cry of recognition. Knox finds this cry in the earliest Christian preaching, at Pentecost:

> What tourist does not know the sudden thrill of hearing his own language talked under strange skies? It was that thrill, experienced beyond all reasonable belief, that gave St Peter an audience when he preached his first sermon (*US,* 434).

Having established an identity with his audience, Knox can share his insights with them. His listeners are encouraged to stand in his shoes because they sense that he has stood in theirs. As Philip Caraman has remarked, the "we" of his sermons is not the cliché of the orator; people sense that their difficulties are also his (*OS*, vii). His natural sensibilities were marked by a conviction of his own ordinariness, and his sympathy for others was heightened by his lifelong work as a translator. Knox is able to identify himself with Saint Thérèse or Saint Paul, but he can also share "The Average Man's Doubts about God" that keep him awake at four in the morning (*US*, 166–72). Unbelievers, too, are of the family and claim his empathy:

> Even when there is no bond of common Christianity, we have a vague respect for a man's religion; he is a Buddhist, yes, but he has got hold of something. To have any respect at all for a man's irreligion—that is much harder. And yet he, too, has got hold of something; he believes, as we do, in logical proof; believes, as we do, in historical accuracy; hates, as we do, the very name of superstition (*OS*, 357).

In his appeal to the ordinary experience of his listeners, Knox is addressing their imaginative faculty, inviting them to recognize in these happenings an encounter with God in Christ. What connection can be made between this "imaginative apologetics" and the logical approach Knox takes in *The Belief of Catholics* and in some of his other writings? As Newman has been helpful in underscoring the primacy of imagination in coming to faith, so also he suggests a relationship between the experiential and rational elements of belief. In order for something to be believed, it must be credible to the imagination; however, once that has happened, the belief must be investigated in order to be authenticated. In this way "an impression in the Imagination has become a system or Creed in the Reason."[1] Such an investigation

[1] John Henry Newman, *Fifteen Sermons Preached before the University of Oxford* (1843; repr. of 1871 ed., Westminster, Md.: Christian Classics, 1961), p. 329.

involves, in the case of Christianity, a study of personal tes-
timonies, episodes from the history of Christianity, the acts
of those who have lived this belief authentically in the past,
and the controversies and decrees of the Christian community. Predisposed to accept this evidence as "reliable", the
investigator finds that, unlike scientific logic, it does not
demonstrate necessity; rather, like legal logic, it converges
and coalesces.

Roman Catholic apologetics in the first half of this century
sought to convince with inexorable logic, and, in Knox' es-
timation, strike the modern reader as inhuman (*PGNA,* 11).
Presumably he includes in this judgment his own apologetical efforts; treated in isolation they might give such an impression. But an understanding of his apologetical writings
must also embrace the sermons and conferences in which
he treats such issues of faith more informally. When this
is done, his logical arguments take their place as one part
of an approach to apologetics that is truly convergent and
persuasive because it appeals not only to the intellect but to
the whole person.

To the end of his life, Knox defended the essential place
of the intellect in religion. For the sake of Christianity at
large, Catholic theology should not "haul down the flag of
intellectualism" and betray part of her characteristic witness;
at the same time, intellectual propaganda must not be isolated from moral and spiritual witness (*PGNA,* 15).

This emphasis on the intellect, taken as *part* of a broader
approach to belief, is of particular value in our own day.
Knox suggests that, by a kind of palace revolution, exis-
tential philosophers have threatened to dethrone the intellect; he wonders if the Age of Reason will be succeeded
by an Age of Will (*PGNA,* 34). Perhaps what has come
about is an Age of Experience. The thirst for "experience",
unaccompanied by critical investigation, can lead to tragic

consequences. The unexamined life is not worth living; unexamined experience is not merely worthless, it is dangerous. Ronald Knox could draw on the experience of his listeners with his powerful use of images; so could the Reverend Jim Jones, or Adolf Hitler. Experience must be submitted to critical investigation.

A necessary test of experience for Knox, as for Newman before him, is the authority of the Church. The importance of this aspect of Catholicism is evident in both his life and his writings. In his youth, Knox tried to frame the question in theoretically exclusive terms: experience *or* authority. Yet upon his conversion he did not publish a reasoned defense for the authority of Roman Catholicism; he shared the experiences, and the reflection upon those experiences, which led him to become a Catholic. Years later, in *Difficulties*, he noted that "The wave of experience will always dash you up against the rock of authority, which dashes you back to seek refuge in experience again" (*Dif,* 239).

The teaching authority of the Catholic Church provides an indispensable context for a reasoned reflection on experience. However, a proper investigation of a particular religious tradition must not be limited to a study of decrees and definitions. As Knox shows in *The Belief of Catholics*, it is not enough to examine "The Truths Catholic Hold" and "The Rules Catholics Acknowledge"; one should also consider "The Strength Catholics Receive" and inhale "The Air Catholics Breathe". Knox views the whole of Catholicism as apologetic. His individual talents are employed to mediate the communal witness of the Church.

Corporate witness has a double significance for Knox. In the first place, it represents a final authentication for the investigation of experience. Knowledge is incomplete until it is tested in the sphere of action. The wave of experience dashes us up against the rock of authority; the system or creed that emerges dashes us back onto the waves of praxis. For this reason, Knox constantly urges believers to *live* their faith. For example, at the end of the every summer term, he would encourage the Oxford undergraduates to enter into the corporate life of their home parishes, "not just to be the kind of Catholic who is seen slinking off to Mass every Sunday at the Oratory or at the Cathedral, a lost unit in the crowd" (*US,* 149). It is not enough for their knowledge to be theoretical; it must be experiential.

The second point about the Church's communal witness is that it must be expressed in the lives of individual believers. Knox reminds his students that their lives will be the illustration, for better or for worse, of the Catholic creed; others will seek in them the real mark of the Church for which the world hungers—the mark of a transformed life (*US,* 64, 234).

Here we encounter Ronald Knox' most convincing apologetic argument: his own life. More significant than his clever arguments or penetrating images is the testimony of a life transformed by the Gospel. The brilliance that expressed itself in so many literary forms finds its integration in his belief. Knox aids others in integrating God's gift with the rest of their living by sharing the integration of his own life. He does so unobtrusively; one finds him to be not only an apologist but a spiritual director and a friend as well. Father Caraman, who edited three volumes of his sermons, notes that they seldom contain a reference to their author: "Mgr Knox was convinced that the preacher should not obtrude himself into his subject" (*OS,* ix). Explicitly, no; but one feels when reading any of these sermons that Knox is speaking of something he has made his own.

PART THREE

SHARING THE TREASURE: THE APOLOGETICS OF RONALD KNOX

INTRODUCTION

Apologetics was at the heart of Ronald Knox' ministry and had an important place in his writings. As chaplain at Oxford and Aldenham and in many of his works for the general public, he sought to make the Christian faith both intelligible and attractive. That apologetics remained a priority in his later life may be seen from his desire to undertake a fresh approach to the subject. In his introduction to *Proving God*, Knox suggests the direction to be taken by some future ideal apologist:

> What I am concerned with is our apologetics, and that great work of apologetics, some day to be written, which shall suggest to the reader that in approaching Christian theology he is approaching something that is alive, not a series of diagrams (*PGNA*, 16).

He then offers a thumbnail sketch of the impact of this approach on five basic questions of apologetics: the existence of God, the Old Testament as prophecy, the Person of Christ, the New Testament as a reliable record, and the Church as authorized teacher. These questions held center stage for Ronald Knox throughout his life, and they remain central to any consideration of Catholic faith today.

This fivefold structure will be used in examining Knox' own apologetics. Each chapter will conclude with a previously unpublished conference by Ronald Knox, found among his papers at Mells. It is to be hoped that this will demonstrate that in some measure he matches his description of the ideal apologist: "Everything will come alive at his touch; he will not merely know what he is talking about, but feel what he is talking about" (*PGNA,* 17).

"TO PROVE THAT GOD IS, AND WHAT GOD IS": THE EXISTENCE OF GOD

The first task of the apologist is

> to prove that God is, and what God is, not merely with the
> effect of intellectual satisfaction, but with a glow of assent
> that springs from the whole being; "did not our hearts burn
> within us when he talked to us by the way?" (*PGNA,* 16).

Knox accepts this starting point of traditional Catholic apologetics, "for, after all, a man may not unreasonably want to be assured that God exists before he will consult Church or Bible to find out more about him" (*GA,* 39). In his approach to this question, Knox can appear to be more concerned with "intellectual satisfaction" than with "a glow of assent". Certainly this is true of his earlier works, *The Belief of Catholics, Broadcast Minds*, and *In Soft Garments*, in which he was responding to the charge that to embrace Catholicism was to commit intellectual suicide. It should be kept in mind, however, that in many conferences and sermons Knox does aim at touching not only the minds but also the hearts of his hearers. In studying his apologetics, this wider body of writings must not be ignored.

In the first part of this chapter, Knox' arguments for the existence of God will be presented; his understanding of the problems involved in accepting God's existence will be treated in the second part; the final section will show how Knox tries to engage the whole person by presenting the implications of God's existence for the individual.

Arguments for the Existence of God

"Must there not be something slightly inhuman about the textbook treatment which hands out the doctrine of God's existence as if it were an investigation into the square root of minus one?" (*PGNA*, 15). It is with this *caveat* that Knox' reflections on God's existence must be read: he is well aware that intellectual argument is only one part of Christian testimony. All too often, its effect has been spoiled by isolating it from the moral and spiritual witness Christians must bear (*PGNA*, 15).

How does Knox defend the "reasonableness" of God's existence? He begins by considering an approach popular in the 1920s: the fact of inner mystical experiences points to an external divine reality. He questions the probative value of this argument from religious experience; even in his later work, which manifests greater sympathy for the mystical approach to God, Knox observes:

> The man who, when a theological assertion is being discussed, slaps his chest and tells us that he "feels it in here," neither produces nor deserves to produce conviction. We have become too suspicious of those matted roots of unconscious to be impressed by the mention of a merely psychological certitude (*PGNA*, 32).

In *The Belief of Catholics*, he employs a whimsical image to illustrate the danger of attempting to demonstrate an external reality from an inner experience:

If a musical enthusiast, after listening to some rare but gay piece, should tell me that as he listened he could actually see elves and gnomes dancing before his eyes, I should be perfectly prepared to reverence both his own superior sensitiveness to musical impressions, and the subtle power of the art which could evoke such an imaginative experience. I should not suppose that elves or gnomes had been present, unseen to myself. And I confess that if I lacked the sense of religion quite so thoroughly as I lack that of music, the disclosures of the mystic would leave me in very much the same position (*BC,* 45).

He also considers a variation of this argument, one which was more persuasive forty years ago than today: the practical universality of belief in God. According to this contention, a person should believe in God because virtually everyone does, "an argument not differing much in principle from the economics of that famous country, whose inhabitants lived by taking in one another's washing" (*BC,* 47). Again, Knox objects that one cannot argue from a state of mind (individual or collective) to a reality that that state of mind presupposes. At best, the phenomenon of religion in various cultures and the evidence of mystical experiences present a challenge to consider whether there are grounds for believing in God's existence.

Knox prefers to demonstrate the existence of God by considering the evidence in creation, which he sees as a crossword puzzle (*US,* 5) and "the oldest detective story in the world".[1] Daily experience numbs us to the amazing fact of creation; what we take for granted is really the most challenging mystery of all. That God should choose to create

[1] Ronald Knox, *Retreat for Beginners* (New York: Sheed and Ward, 1960), p. 46.

anything outside himself is "much the most difficult dogma of the Christian system" (*OR,* 24).

The "why" of the world is elusive; the "what" of the world bears testimony to its Author. In all his apologetic writings, Knox holds that the central argument for the existence of God is to be found in the traditional Scholastic "Five Ways".[2] He supplements these with other evidence —such as the phenomenon of conscience—and his judgment of the relative merits of each of the five approaches changes, but they remain central to his demonstration of God's existence.

He is well aware that this metaphysical approach is difficult. Most people cannot follow a course of abstract reasoning without a certain sense of suffocation, and the seeker after the faith of childhood pleads, "Cannot I retrace my steps without these forced marches over barren and unfamiliar scenery? Is there no short cut to the religion of gentle Jesus, and the certitude of the Sunday School?" (*PGNA,* 51). This "barren" avenue is not simply preferable; it is indispensable, as being the only one left open by those who question God's existence. Julian Huxley, in his *Religion without*

---

[2] "The five 'ways' or arguments by which St. Thomas Aquinas (*Summa Theol.* I, q. 2, art. 3) sought to prove the existence of God *a posteriori*, i.e. from effects of His which are known to us. Aquinas' arguments conclude that (1) change (*motus*) implies a first unchanging changer; (2) that a sequence of efficient causes, and their effects, such as we find in the world, implies an uncaused first cause; (3) that the existence of things able to be generated and to perish implies the existence of what is not generable and perishable (i.e. 'necessary') and that the existence of what is necessary ultimately implies the existence of something the existence of which derives from nothing apart from itself; (4) that the comparisons we make (more or less 'true', 'good', 'noble', etc.) imply a standard of comparison which is itself perfect in all these qualities; (5) that the fulfillment by inanimate or unintelligent objects of an end to which they invariably tend implies the existence of a purpose or intelligence operative in nature." "Quinque Viae", in *Oxford Dictionary of the Christian Church,* 3rd ed.

Revelation, claims that there is next to no evidence of God's existence. Knox asks in response what conceivable kind of evidence would carry weight with Huxley. He has ruled out miracles as intrinsically impossible; religious experiences are explained as rooted in the subconscious. What is left, Knox wonders, except the evidence derived from the facts of existence as we know them, such as the presence of order in nature? The response to this evidence is that Huxley is "bored by metaphysics": " 'Idle speculation,' he calls it. I wonder if it has ever occurred to him that the refusal to speculate may be a mark of idleness?"[3]

Knox does not shirk the task of speculation. In his apologetics, he seeks to breathe life into the dry bones of metaphysical arguments for God's existence. He presents the "Five Ways" in *The Belief of Catholics* (*BC,* 48–50), and he refers to them in *The Creed in Slow Motion* (*CSM,* 14), but it is above all in his Oxford conferences that we find Knox drawing out the implications of the Scholastic arguments. These conferences also reflect the evolution of his thought concerning the relative merits of the "proofs".

In his earlier conferences, his preference is for the demonstration of God's existence from the order found in nature. The mysteries that science seeks to unravel and the principles that research discovers are elements of the "crossword of creation", and a crossword that a mind can solve requires a Mind to make it up. Order is "the cipher by which Mind speaks to mind in the midst of chaos" (*US,* 5). He finds in this Mind not only the explanation for the laws of nature but for the fact of creation itself. The alternative to this ordering Mind is blind chance, which Knox rejects as involving too many coincidences. "Accident is all right as an explanation

---

[3] Ronald Knox, *Broadcast Minds* (London: Sheed and Ward, 1932), p. 57.

at first, but there comes a point at which the thing begins to look like carelessness" (*US*, 7). He also questions the validity of moving from chance as an explanation for the *possibility* of the world as we know it to the *fact* of the world itself:

> If the police were to discover a human body in Lord [Bertrand] Russell's Saratoga trunk, he would not be able to satisfy them with the explanation that, among all the innumerable articles of luggage in the world, it is only natural that there should be some few which are large enough to contain a body. They would want to know how it got there (*US*, 7).

Finally, even if countless random encounters of atoms could explain the origin and evolution of the physical world, there remains the question of a "new order of existence" represented by the human mind. Can matter develop itself into mind? For Knox, this is "a hopeless metaphysical contradiction" (*US*, 8). This line of thought is developed in a radio broadcast on the subject, "What I Believe":

> Even if a man can sit down under the stupendous fact of material nature without recognising in its ordered processes the work of an intelligent Creator, I do not see how he sits down under this major miracle, the wedding and welding of body and spirit in our nature; that all these millions of biological specimens we call men should exist, each of them, as it were, a reflecting mirror that catches a light not its own; each capable of providing an audience for the great theatre of experience, even if no other human being lived to share it— that this should have happened of its own accord in a universe dedicated to the achievement of merely statistical results, is a thing—let me stick to my terms of reference—past all my powers of believing.[4]

[4] Ronald Knox, "What I Believe", in *What I Believe: Broadcast Talks*, ed. A. D. Ritchie et al. (London: Porcupine Press, 1948), pp. 30–31.

As rational creatures, men are "the *enfant terrible* of Natural History, a cuckoo's egg in the nest of bewildered Creation."[5]

The relation between "matter" and "mind" elicits further reflection from Knox in a subsequent conference. Existence as we experience it is divided exactly in half: one half being the things we know, the other half being our mind knowing them. In many ways, mind is dependent on matter. The mind can only receive its impressions and express itself through a mysterious liaison with its material body: drunkenness, indigestion, a blow to the head affect the life of the mind through the life of the body. Also, mind seems in some way unnecessary. If somehow all minds ceased to exist, the world would continue on quite happily, "with white ants or octopuses or something occupying the position of nature's darling instead of man" (*US*, 10).

Yet the very dependency of mind on matter paradoxically implies its superiority. We can conceive of the brain existing for the sake of thinking; we cannot conceive of thinking existing for the sake of the brain. Matter is the servant of mind. And, unlike matter, which can only be the object of thought, mind can be both object and subject. The human mind is self-conscious, aware of itself as thinking. This self-consciousness is experienced as something personal. Thus, when we conceive of God as a "Mind", we are speaking not of an abstraction but of a Person.

Knox underlines this personal aspect of God by a clever twist. He notes that "matter" and "mind" are not only nouns but also verbs: things matter, people mind. Here he argues for the existence of God on the testimony of conscience: "Can anything matter, unless there is Somebody who minds?"

[5] Ronald Knox, *The Beginning and the End of Man* (London: Catholic Truth Society, 1921), p. 4.

(*US,* 13). Right and wrong ultimately must not be abstractions, like "duty". They must derive from the will of a personal Lawgiver who has the right to "mind": "But if there were no *he*, if there were only an *it*, to dictate commands to free moral beings like ourselves, could we reconcile ourselves to the indignity of it? I know I couldn't" (*US,* 14).

The argument from conscience is developed in another conference. When considering what is "good" (or true or beautiful), a fixed point is needed. Is it conscience that makes things good, the mind that makes them true, intuition that makes them beautiful? Both history and daily experience indicate how variable human judgments are on these basic questions. If God is the source of Goodness, Truth, and Beauty, then he is the fixed point needed. Knox cautions that this line of thought does not testify necessarily to God's existence, but only to our wanting him to exist. And there is the added danger of conceiving a very inadequate understanding of God, as a sort of backdrop to our lives, whereas,

If once you prove he exists, you will find that he fills the whole stage. Man is no longer the centre of the Universe —God is the centre of the Universe. . . . All the greatness of man, all his splendid achievements in art and in music and in learning and in the conquest of nature, in law and governments, in heroism and endurance, fade away into the background and become something very insignificant, when they are seen in contrast with the incommunicable Majesty of Almighty God (*US,* 19).

Insignificant perhaps when contrasted with the majesty of God, it was nonetheless a human achievement that caused Knox to question his easy reliance on the argument from order in creation. The scientific discoveries involved in the production of the atomic bomb called for a reevaluation of

"Thomism and Atomism" (*GA*, 34–50). In his later Oxford conferences, Knox is more circumspect in his use of the Scholastic proofs.

In one of these talks, he poses the question, "Does proof matter?" Reviewing the profound revolutions in thought from the thirteenth century to our own, he concludes: "We do not live in a bay sheltered from every wind that blows; the currents of contemporary thought do create their backwash among ourselves, cherish as we may our own certitudes" (*US*, 162). Even the distinction between believer and unbeliever can be blurred. There are times when every believer feels the attraction of atheism: "You and I have got all the apparatus in us for doubting every article of the Christian creed; faith is not a knife which cuts them [doubts] out; it is an injection which neutralizes them" (*US*, 166).

It is this experience of the questioning believer lying awake at four in the morning that prompts Knox to re-examine the "five proofs". The two proofs that were most satisfactory in youth were those from Motion and Cause, perhaps because students have had the experience of pushing in line and of passing the blame when accused. Knox now finds these the more vulnerable. The weak link comes in the argument from a natural effect to a supernatural cause. To this objection,

> I don't . . . suggest that there isn't a comeback. I only say that the whole argument resolves itself into a discussion about whether metaphysics exist at all, and people start talking about the blind man in the dark room looking for the black cat that isn't there. That is the point in the discussion at which I slide out of the room and say I've got to put out the vestments for tomorrow (*US*, 169).

Here he makes an important shift in his use of the Scholastic proofs. He invites the students to put aside the question whether the existence of God can be proved by direct logical inference from our knowledge of the world around us. Rather, we should ask whether the existence of God is not an apprehension that comes to us in and through our knowledge of the world and still more through our knowledge of ourselves:

> I am suggesting that the knowledge of God is something which emerges from our knowledge of life, although for the life of us we can't quite see how it got there. Does that sound wholly paradoxical? Tell me, then, how do we get our notion of solid objects, when we can only see in two dimensions? How do we get our notion of reality, when our experience consists of nothing but a series of sense-impressions? How do we get our notion of right and wrong, when our natural faculties of appreciation only tell us that some things are fun and some aren't? How is it that we always find ourselves putting a construction on our experience which isn't exactly part of that experience, yet obviously isn't something we just *put* there? (*US,* 170).

In order to look at the world sanely, it must be seen as something deriving its existence and meaning from Something outside of and higher than itself. The "five ways" and other arguments can be understood as a series of tests to assure us that the God-dependent construction we put on the universe is correct (*US,* 170). This approach brings Knox back to the majesty of God, seen now not in contrast to human achievement but as reflected in it:

> If the doctrine of Creation is a guess man's mind was made to leap at, a spark that flies unbidden from the anvil of experience, then you get a different angle on the whole process. Then there is no time-lag between your discerning that God

exists, and the reflection that you ought to do something about it. You apprehend, with one grasp of the mind, earth's inadequacy and God's all-sufficiency; you see yourself, earthborn, in the true perspective, and read, written in between the lines of all our human record, the attestation of a God whom to acknowledge is to adore (*US,* 172).

In later life, Knox believed the third argument, from contingent to necessary Being, would receive the most favorable hearing in a world that had passed from the Newtonian order of the eighteenth century through Darwinism in the nineteenth century to the Relativism of the atomic age. In his final apologetic work, Knox returns to this argument from contingent and necessary Being. What, he asks, is the strange plus-quality that makes the difference between the imaginary chimera and the hardly less improbable platypus? Better yet, he invites the reader to take himself as a type of actuality:

I should be surprised if Mr. Pickwick came into the room; why am I not surprised to find myself in the room? The problem, if you come to think of it, is the same. Pickwick was projected into the world by Dickens, but as an idea only— man could do no more. By what means, then, am I projected into the world, an actuality? (*PGNA,* 39).

The source of this actuality can be found in God who *is,* who alone exists in his own right. This apprehension is conjointly the work of the intellect and the will: the apex of human thought is the knowledge of God, the apex of human desire is the love of God. In Knox' final work, the cloud of suspicion has lifted from the world of mystical experience:

It may be that the theologian and the mystic are like two climbers, each making the ascent of the same peak, but at a little distance from one another. So intent is each on his own difficult progress, that he has no time to look round at the steps his neighbour has carved in the snow. No reason to blame either, until either begins to blame the other for not following in his footsteps (*PGNA,* 40).

By the argument from contingent being, the theologian has come to know what the mystic has come to feel, utter dependence on a Reality outside himself.

The challenge Ronald Knox faced in demonstrating the existence of God involved putting the case in such a way that it would have intellectual integrity and also overcome the aridity that reduces metaphysics to mathematics. It would not be enough, Knox learned, to produce conviction; the apologist must aim at conversion:

> Oh, the argument shall be all according to the books, as scholastic as you will. But the diagram which illustrates the argument shall be the reader himself; in his own mind, how important, and yet, even to his own mind, how inadequate! He is not lost in a maze of abstractions; it is of his very real self that we speak. His whole sympathies are engaged by the argument; he is like the land forces of Athens in Sicily, following, with the unconscious motions of their bodies, the progress of the sea-battle. The argument shall convince him purely as an argument; but when it does so, it shall find him on his knees (*PGNA,* 42).

Obstacles to Belief

The ingenuity of Knox' arguments paradoxically underscores the fact that belief in God does not come easily. What are some of the obstacles which prevent a "God-dependent" understanding of the world and of ourselves? This is the subject of the conference at the end of this chapter, but it is a question he deals with frequently.

Knox identifies three attitudes that paralyze the search for God from the outset. For some, the progress of human achievement pushes the presence of God out of their consciousness:

> Because our promised land flows with pasteurized milk and synthetic honey, we forget where the raw materials came from, and so we are in danger of forgetting who it was that gave them, and what he asks of us (*OS,* 374).

A second type of complacency affects those who do not really believe because it has never occurred to them to doubt whether God exists. There are, thirdly, those who do not look for God because they do not want to find him; the recognition of his existence would interfere with their pleasures and ambitions (*Dif,* 210; *PGNA,* 43).

The search for God once begun, the great obstacle to belief is the problem of evil:

> Let me remind you, first, what a pivotal difficulty this problem of suffering is. I should say that nine in every ten of the people who describe themselves as atheists ought really to be described, more accurately, as pessimists. They have not examined the proofs for the existence of God, and found them wanting. They have simply looked round on the world, with all its tragedies, its miseries, its inequalities, and asked themselves how such an organization of the world can possibly be consistent with the rule of an all-powerful and a beneficent Providence.[6]

The fact of evil challenges either the power or the goodness of God. The most difficult article in the Creed is the first one: "God the Father Almighty" (*CSM,* 19). The God

[6] Ronald Knox, "Suffering", typescript, ca. 1934, Mells. , Somerset. Text may be found in Milton Walsh, *Ronald Knox as Apologist* (S.T.D. diss., Gregorian University, Rome, 1985), pp. 448–61.

of Knox is almighty; it is unthinkable that "such a Creator could lose control of his own handiwork" (*Dif,* 152). A "limited" God is not worthy of worship (*Dif,* 158). He cautions the schoolgirls at Aldenham against conceiving of God as powerless to prevent suffering: "You mustn't think of him as a kind of amiable Official up in heaven who is really very sorry about it, but he's afraid nothing can be done" (*CSM,* 20).

But when nothing *is* done, where is God's goodness? A partial answer to this mystery can be found in the doctrine of free will. If God intervened every time man was about to harm another, free will would be a farce (*CSM,* 24). The possibility of evil is the flip side of the coin of virtue:

> Moral goodness as we know it can only exist under conditions of struggle, and against a background of evil. We are so shut in with the world of our own experience, that any other kind of moral goodness is inaccessible to our imaginations (*OS,* 333).

Our experience of moral goodness requires the possibility of evil; so, Knox suggests, God created the possibility of evil, and we actualized it (*OS,* 333). This actualization has made us misfits, exiles. We are like "some noble beast in captivity, that grows accustomed to its prison bars, yet never ceases to chafe at them" (*PS,* 276). The point of the account of the Fall in Genesis is that we were made for a destiny we have missed:

> To do, all the time, the things you don't approve of yourself for doing; to be, all the time, something you wish you weren't—what destiny could be more ludicrous? You might as well be a carnivorous rabbit. Man is a fallen creature, the free will he enjoys, which was meant to be a kind of parachute that would enable him to float among the clouds, has turned

inside out, and is no better than an umbrella to keep the rain off him here and there.[7]

But is it fair that future generations are penalized for some primeval Fall? Knox responds that our present condition should not be understood as a penalty but as the withdrawal of certain gifts:

> To give a very crude parallel; it is not as if a school-master said, "You will all write 200 lines every day this term, to punish the insolence of last term's sixth form (who have now left) in writing their names on the seats in my garden." It is rather as if he said, "I am not going to let you wander about in my garden in future, because when I gave that privilege to your predecessors they misused it" (*OR,* 26).

Granted that God respects man's free will, it may still be asked why he respects it so much. Why do the wicked prosper? If the justice of God were more clearly reflected in the world, both his existence and his goodness would be more manifest. In Knox' opinion, such frequent visitations of divine judgment would produce a slave-mentality among most people:

> We should behave like schoolboys . . . , who cannot indeed *see* that the master is in the room, but know that he is in the room because he always hits them on the back of the head if they try to look up from their books (*Dif,* 211).

Free will accounts for some suffering, but how can we make sense of the evil that is not the fruit of human malice? We cannot. The suffering brought about by disease or natural catastrophes cannot be "explained". Such suffering can be given a meaning, as a manifestation of discipline or a

[7] Ronald Knox, "Why Does God Make Sin So Easy and Goodness So Difficult?" in *Asking Them Questions: A Selection from the Three Series,* ed. by Ronald Selby Wright (London: Oxford University Press, 1953), p. 165.

share in the sufferings of Christ in the work of redemption. And belief in God offers the consolation that if some suffer more than others, there must be compensation in the world to come.

The reality of such evil underscores the fact that on earth, God's will is at work secretly, under the conditions of mystery, and that faith is needed to discern it (*PS,* 14). Providence is not something that is seen; rather, we believe there must be providence at work, because God is good. But how do we know that he is good?

> Long ago, in a book which nobody reads now, I did write an essay in the character of a Modernist clergyman, which was called "Canon Dives' explanation of the existence of Good." And he explained, of course, that without the existence of good there would be no possibility of evil. It worked out right on paper; why is it nonsense? Because whatever else we are uncertain about, we are certain that good is the positive thing, and evil the negative thing, just as light is the positive thing and darkness is the negative thing; evil does not exist in its own right, but only as the privation of good. And because God *is*, God is good and not evil. Somehow, his own character must be reflected, both in his creation of the world and his ordering of it (*OS,* 334).

Implications of God's Existence

In the figure of the Prodigal Son, Knox finds an image of our human condition after the Fall; we are sojourners in a strange land "where only man goes wanting, and the beasts have their fill" (*PS,* 213). Even in the depths of sin, the idea of God haunts us:

> What is this hunger for food which only becomes articulate at the sight of beasts feeding, and then expresses itself in a

hunger for home? It is the hunger of the immortal soul for God; he has made us for himself, and our hearts cannot rest until they find rest in him. The soul that has plunged into vicious habits, and seems so deeply sunk in them, now, that there is no chance for recovery, still finds itself dissatisfied with the brief enjoyments, the narrow horizons, of earth. . . . And then, on a rebound, the half-repentant mind turns away from the beast-world that surrounds it to the angel-world from which it came out, and which must for ever be its goal. "How many of my father's servants" . . . was not that service, after all, perfect freedom? (*PS,* 213–14).

"Was not that service perfect freedom?" In these few words, Knox sums up the pivotal meaning of God's existence for us. Because our existence depends on his, the goal of our lives must be to glorify God. Prosperity or misery, success or failure, none of these matter, so long as God is glorified in us. This service means perfect freedom especially to ordinary people and to those who feel they are useless:

God created you for his glory. That ought to be very consoling to some of us. Some of us, I mean, aren't doing anything very important in life and aren't likely to; just adding up figures at a desk or sweeping floors—it doesn't make any difference. If you're doing the work that's given you for the glory of God your work is just as important as the Prime Minister's. And it ought to be a consolation to those of us whom ill-health has knocked out of life's battle altogether, so that God seems to have no work for us to do except to lie still and suffer; their work is still important as anybody else's, if they will devote their sufferings to God's glory (*US,* 364).

The purpose of any human effort must be ultimately not our satisfaction but God's praise. Every person ought to live in such a way that "your will should be a clear pool in which his will is mirrored, a perfectly attuned instrument which shall sound in harmony with his."[8]

The God who lies at the end of our human reasoning is the Lord of Creation, worthy to receive the praise of his creatures. But he is also the God who has revealed that he does not call us servants, but friends. While this chapter has concerned itself with Knox' natural theology, it would be incomplete if mention were not made of the twin mysteries of God's love for us and our love for him.

In a sermon on the Blessed Sacrament, Knox speaks of two staggering affirmations that the Christian religion involves, compared with which all the other doctrines are easy to assimilate: (1) God cares for everybody; (2) God cares for me. He explores the implication of these two simple statements:

> You pass through the streets as you go to your daily work, and see all those thousands of your fellow beings—faces hardened by money-getting, faces impudent with the affectation of vice, faces vacant with frivolity, faces lined with despair—and it seems to you impossible that each one of those faces, with so little recognition in it of a divine vocation or an eternal destiny, can yet represent a soul for which God cares. And yet he does care, if theology is to mean anything; cares for this one as he cares for Zaccheus, cares for that one as he cared for Mary Magdalen, cares for that one as he cared for the rich young man, cares for that one as he cared for the penitent thief. All these millions of human souls, and he cares for each, thirsts for each. And then suddenly you think of your own soul, only one among all those millions, and among all those millions so little distinguishable by really vivid faith, by really generous love, by real intimacy with the things of eternity; can it really be, you ask yourself, that he cares for me? (*PS,* 303).

[8] Ronald Knox, *Anglican Cobwebs* (London: Sheed and Ward, 1928), p. 49.

What Knox underlines here is the profoundly personal nature of God's care for each of us. This goes beyond the general providence of creation and constitutes an invitation to receive this love and reciprocate. God's love draws us like a magnet; our hearts turn to him as flowers follow the sun, "not persuaded by reason, but drawn upwards by a native impulse."[9]

Centuries of Christian preaching have familiarized people with the idea of our loving God. Knox points out the novelty of this theme by quoting Aristotle: "We should think it very odd to hear anybody talking about loving Zeus" (*US*, 191 quoting Aristotle, *Magna Moralia*, bk. 2, chap. 11, l. 32). Even in the Old Testament, the theme of loving God plays a relatively minor role; it is only mentioned about thirty times. For the most part, talk of loving God is New Testament language. Christians are "the spoilt children of revelation" who "take it as the most natural thing in the world that God should want us to love him, instead of reminding ourselves that it is the most amazing act of condescension on his part".[10]

Two sayings from a notebook kept by Knox may well sum up his reflections on the existence of God. Regarding his dependence on God, he wrote: "*Ex te et per te sum; in te et ad te sim*".[11] (I exist from you and through you; may I be in you and for you.) And after years of apologetic writing, he summed up his understanding of God in this way: "I am reminded of an unfinished sentence when I try to focus upon the thought of God. Whether this is right, I don't know."[12]

[9] Ronald Knox, *Layman and His Conscience* (New York: Sheed and Ward, 1961), p. 36.

[10] *Layman and His Conscience*, p. 34.

[11] "Sayings of Mgr R. A. Knox", *The Month* (Aug. 1959): 109.

[12] Ibid, p. 110.

AGNOSTICISM AND BELIEF

The conferences this term are devoted to considering whether, and if so by what arguments, the existence of God can
be proved. No discussion of this subject has gone very far before you come up against the difficulty, "If it can be proved,
how are we to account for the existence of the agnostic who
doubts, and the atheist who denies, every statement we make
about the supernatural world?" Are they very stupid people,
who cannot see the point of an argument? Or are they very
wicked people, who for some ulterior purpose of their own
insist on turning a blind eye to our telescope? That is the
main problem which confronts us this morning, a problem
(you may say) of psychology. Behind it lies a problem of
theology, "Is it possible to be an atheist or an agnostic in
good faith, even when the arguments for the existence of
God have been fully and competently expounded to you?"
About that, perhaps, we will say a little; but it really lies
outside our present terms of reference.

There are plenty of people who claim to be theists, and
even claim to be Christians, without admitting that the existence of God can be the subject of rational proof. And these
people, for various reasons, are not worried when they meet
an agnostic, or hear an atheist speaking in Hyde Park; it seems
to them the most natural thing in the world that such contradictions of their own belief should be found, and found
commonly. I would like to develop that point, if I may, for
a moment or two.

I would divide these people into two classes, labeling the
one "sub-Christian", and the other "ultra-Christian". The

Ronald Knox, "Agnosticism and Belief", conference, typescript, n.d. Knox
Papers, Mells, Somerset.

sub-Christian is a person who knows all about the arguments for the existence of God—or so he says—and he
makes no attempt to disturb our simple faith in them; he
just says they don't "convince" him. If you question him,
and suggest that he has, perhaps, an immediate perception
of God's existence, like the immediate perception he has of
his own existence, he disclaims the imputation at once; no,
nothing of that kind. He can only tell you that after all you
have got to interpret the universe and human life one way
or the other, on a religious basis or on a materialist basis,
and to him the religious basis seems more satisfactory; it
goes, on the whole, with disciplined thought and upright
living. Perhaps, if you press him very hard, he will point
you to the mystical writers and suggest that they, after all,
are the supreme artists in this matter of religion; and he is
content to go by their guidance, as he would be content to
go by the guidance of a person with highly developed taste
in judging of music, for example, or of painting.

Now, a man like that may have a quarrel to pick with the
atheist, whom he regards as at best a tiresome dogmatist,
at the worst a disturber of the peace. But with the agnostic
he hits it off well enough. Both of them think of argument
on the subject of religion as somehow an error of taste; it
is harnessing the human reason to a use for which it was
never intended. Both alike have a gentle horror of fanaticism.
The only thing which makes a difference between them is
that the agnostic has adopted the materialist interpretation
of life as a provisional hypothesis, and finds that it answers
to his expectations. There is nothing very surprising in that;
it takes all sorts to make a world. "You, Socrates, think this
way, and I that"—it is a case for intellectual coexistence.
As for the idea that a man who is, from your point of view,
religiously tone-deaf should be regarded as guilty in some

way of a moral failing—that simply does not cross the mind of the sub-Christian; why should it?

The person whom I have described, rather audaciously perhaps, as the ultra-Christian refuses to argue about the existence of God for quite different reasons. To him, brought up in the strict Evangelical tradition, the doctrine of God's existence is essentially a part of revelation; it comes to him with a feeling of warm, personal assurance as an element in that message of salvation which bounds the whole of his spiritual horizon. You get that in Pascal; Pascal admits that the five scholastic proofs are valid, but he says it's useless and worse than useless to convince a man by the use of those proofs unless you can at the same time convince him of sin, of his need for a Redeemer. Worse than useless, because he will go on sinning, and now he won't have any excuse; he won't be able to plead that he didn't believe in God and therefore couldn't have been expected to do better. But of course on the whole this ultra-Christian dislike of natural theology is a Protestant tendency, going back to the false idea of grace which came in with the Reformation. You dislike natural theology simply because it is natural; nothing that isn't supernatural is any good. All this business has flared up again in our day with the Existentialists; it makes Karl Barth furious if you try to prove the existence of God; you can't prove it, it's a matter of revelation. (Never, by the way, tell yourself that such and such an idea, which you regard as superstitious, is for that reason bound to die out. Superstition is native to the human mind, and it is always recurring.)

It is easy to see that for the ultra-Christian, as for the sub-Christian, there is no difficulty about accounting for the existence of agnosticism or about determining the guilt of those who profess it. On his view, to believe in God is simply part of the unreasoning act of faith by which you accept belief in Jesus Christ. You go to the revival meeting, and the man says "stand up all those who accept Christ" (or whatever the phrase may be), and if you don't stand up it is your fault—you have missed your opportunity. You've got to open your mouth and shut your eyes; there's no need to beat about the bush, hunting for arguments.

Notoriously, we Catholics are in a more difficult position. Because we have to believe, as a matter of faith, the article included in the decrees of the [First] Vatican Council, "If anybody says that we cannot have certain knowledge of the one true God by the light of human reason, let him by anathema". It is true, we are only committed to the view that such knowledge can be attained, not to any particular view about how it is attained, still less to the view that the arguments in question do in fact appear convincing, when properly stated, to every human mind. Like Dr Johnson, we are bound to provide our questioner with arguments, we are not bound to provide him with sufficient intelligence to understand them. All the same, it does seem odd that if these arguments are as copper-bottomed as the Vatican Council says they are, they should so often miss their mark. Here is Professor So-and-so, who is paid to understand about philosophy, and he won't look at them. Here is my friend So-and-so, a decent-living man and no fool, who's in love with a Catholic girl and longs to be a Catholic himself, but he can't make head or tail of them. Meanwhile, our critics have no difficulty in explaining the situation to us. "Nobody" they say "was ever convinced by the arguments for God's existence unless he believed in God already. The trouble about you Christians is that you've got a kind of mystical,

intuitive perception of God, only you're too muddled to realize it, or too dishonest to admit it. So you try to rationalize this intuition of yours in terms of cause and motion and
contingent being and all the rest of it. But what interests us
is your belief, not your rationalizations. Why not give up
trying to argue about it?''

Well, two can play at that game; and if your friend goes
home after the argument convinced that you've been ratio-
nalizing, you go away equally convinced that he has. Not
that you suspect him of having a mystical intuition about
the non-existence of God: but you do suspect him of ulterior motives—just as he thinks you were predisposed to
believe in the scholastic arguments, you think he was predisposed to disbelieve in them, or preindisposed to believe
in them, if you like to put it in that way. If he doesn't believe
in the existence of God, it's really because he doesn't want
God to exist. It's a moral barrier, not an intellectual one,
that divides you. Not that you suspect him of bad faith; he
does quite honestly imagine that his objections are intellectual ones. But it is so easy, isn't it, to be deceived about
that kind of thing. Somehow, the recognition of a Supreme
Being wouldn't fit into the moral pattern of his life; what
seemed an intellectual denial was a moral refusal.

That is, I suppose, the conventional account of the matter.
The text-books always leave you with the impression that
if a man who enjoys the use of his reason doesn't recognize
and worship a God, that is his *fault*. And if it is his fault,
then there must be some motive underlying his revolt from
theology. What motive? It isn't difficult to see that several
might be operative. First of all, just idleness, the common-
est of human failings. Not necessarily the mere bodily inertia which shrinks from turning over a printed page and
finding out what it is all about, but a kind of mental inertia

which makes it possible to treat something which we read as entirely remote from ourselves; to give it what Newman would have called a merely notional assent. In old days, you couldn't take your degree at Cambridge without passing an examination in Paley's Evidences of Christianity; but I imagine a great many young men must have got it up solidly so as to make sure of passing, without even considering whether the argument held water or not. Some of us, perhaps, did apologetics at school rather in the same spirit. There must, I suppose, be people who were given the grace to find out the truth about religion, and missed their chance simply because it seemed too much like work. An uncomfortable picture; a bit like ourselves, don't you think?

And then there's pride. The ultra-Christian, the man we were talking about just now, puts down all irreligion to pride, and from his point of view that's understandable; if accepting Christ is such a total leap in the dark as he wants it to be, and insists that it shall be, then to ask for proof of any kind is evidently pride; you are setting up your puny wisdom against the wisdom of your Creator. From our point of view, pride is not nearly so common a barrier to belief in the supernatural. But there are people, I think—people of our age, anyhow—who are determined to live their own lives and hate the idea of toeing the line with other men; Outsiders in the making. To them, the whole notion of religion seems something bourgeois and Victorian, to have your liberty of choice cramped by a set of rules which claim their sanction in eternity is to add one more link to the fetters which bind the human race. And a person like that can't look with straight eyes at any evidence which points to the existence of a Supreme Being; it is distorted for him by the unconscious propaganda of egoism.

And then there's plain, honest, moral rebellion. There's

the man who holds no high-falutin' theories about human liberty and the duty of self-realization—he just finds it fun breaking the commandments and doesn't mean to stop. Whether such a man, in the individual case, is in bad faith or not is a thing which only the Divine Wisdom can ascertain; our human guesses on the subject are seldom charitable, and often wide of the mark. I believe it is good modern psychology to say that if you don't want a thing to exist you are liable to throw up a sort of defence-mechanism which assures you that it doesn't exist; how much blame is there in that? It is not for us to say. But the effect of it is just the same as if a man deliberately turned his eyes away from the notion of a Divine Lawgiver for fear he might feel embarrassed when he breaks the Divine Law.

All those are possible barriers to belief, and it isn't always easy to be sure which, in any given case, is operative. I suppose St Augustine, more than any other man, has left the log-book of his conscience to posterity; but can you be quite sure what was wrong, all those years, with St Augustine? It wasn't idleness; I think that's fairly clear. But did he, in his heart of hearts, shrink from the idea of getting rid of his mistress? Or was he an Outsider *manqué*, who failed at the last moment to live his own life? He probably thought it was rather a fine thing to be a Manichean, when the world around him was so contentedly Christian.

Well, are we satisfied with that? The text-books are; they have already shewn us that the arguments in favour of theism are unanswerable; and if so the human mind, being made to apprehend truth, must necessarily apprehend truth here, unless it is unfitted for its office through some outside interference. But I wonder whether we have the right to assume that the human mind, when it comes to judge of such matters, is bound to function so smoothly, so electronically, as all that?

What bothers me is that as you get old, and can look back on the acquaintance you have had with a very large number of your fellow men, it becomes more and more difficult to label your agnostic friends and put them away in a drawer, one marked Idle, another Proud, another Rebellious. In old age, you have to be on your guard against judging people too charitably, just as in youth you have to be on your guard against judging them rashly; I know that. And of course we can't really see inside people's minds. But somehow when it comes to real life, and you fall to wondering why this or that person of your acquaintance is unsusceptible to the influences of religion, the formula just doesn't seem to work. You find it difficult to suppose that this or that individual person is putting up a barrage against the influences of religion, even unconsciously.

What are we to make of it, then? Why, I think, this. The passage from unbelief to belief is, of its nature, an intellectual process. The detonation of it may be a sudden one, as it was with St Augustine, as it was with Mr C. S. Lewis. But you have moved to a position in which you are certain that a God exists—not by any Glory-Hallelujah feeling inside, but with a steady, intellectual conviction. Only you mustn't expect it to happen automatically, with the same painless precision as the demonstration that the angles of a triangle are equal to two right angles. We are engaged in a spiritual adventure, in which the whole of man's nature is concerned; and we need more than a mere absence of bad dispositions if it is to be effected. We need positive good dispositions; there must be a moral preparation in our wills. It is not enough that we should merely conquer sloth; we must be on the alert, ready to follow up the decision of the intellect by action. It is not a mere absence of pride that is called for, but a positive humility which is ready to cry out, "My

Lord and my God". It is not enough that we should have no great attachment to our sins; there must be the dawnings of an unconditional loyalty to the will of God, "Lord, what wilt thou have me do?" Otherwise, the pull of nature will be too strong; we shall recognize, perhaps, the force of an argument, but we shall not have the courage to register our assent; we shall clutch at every straw of doubt, and try, without conscious hypocrisy, to persuade ourselves that it is still possible to suspend judgement.

The agnostic, commonly, is one who shrinks from this act of self-surrender. He has, it may be, scented trouble from afar, and given the propaganda of theism a wide berth so as not to be involved in these complexities. What degree of moral culpability he has incurred, we are in no position to decide. There is no need to represent him as a man who sins against the light; habit and convention and a hundred other remote influences keep him where he is. But the root of his trouble is that he dreads a heroic decision. Most of us, at different levels, have shrunk from heroic decisions before now, and it is not for us to cast a stone at him.

11

"TO VINDICATE THE PROPHECIES":
THE OLD TESTAMENT AS PROPHECY

The second task of Knox' ideal apologist is to "vindicate the prophecies, not by raking up a score of familiar quotations, but by exhibiting the Old Testament *in extenso* as a cipher message imposed on history" (*PGNA,* 16). From his Evangelical upbringing, Ronald Knox received a lifelong passion for the Scriptures, a passion that found expression in his project of producing a new translation of the entire Bible. Whenever he opened the Scriptures, Ronald Knox found himself carried back to the intense curiosity of his childhood: "It is certain that whenever I sit down to read even the simplest story in the Bible, a crowd of questionings, of the Sir-please-Sir-Sir-why-did-he-do-that-Sir? order come flocking into my mind" (*PS,* 350). This fascination for questions raised by the details of biblical stories influenced his interpretation of the Bible; it has been suggested that Knox the exegete had something in common with Knox the detective, reading clues left by the sacred authors overlooked by the professional "Scotland Yard" biblical scholars.[1]

In his spiritual interpretation of Scripture in sermons and retreat conferences, Knox does not hesitate to use figures and events of the Old Testament symbolically. Preaching on

[1] John F. McConnell, "Monsignor Knox, Malleus Exegetarum", *Catholic Biblical Quarterly* (April 1947): 155–69.

various saints, for example, he draws parallels between Saint Edmund and King David, Saint Edward and the just man of Wisdom, Saint Thomas More and Eleazar, the early Jesuits and the Maccabees, even Saint Bernadette and Moses (*OS,* 38, 23, 114, 60, 83). His entire *Retreat for Priests* consists of meditations on Old Testament heroes applied to the priestly life.

Given his personal style of exegesis, his interest in details, and his willingness to apply spiritual meanings to Old Testament events, it is surprising that Knox does not develop any correlation between specific events and their fulfillment in the life of Christ. This is more remarkable in light of his belief that the idea that Christ's life fulfilled in every detail the prophecies constitutes "one of the most impressive arguments you can find in the defence of our holy religion" (*PS,* 476).

Knox did not "rake up" familiar quotations from the Old Testament, but he sought to explore the action of God in human history, above all in the history of the Jews. While recognizing the rationalist prejudice against the possibility of God "putting his oar in, here in this comfortable world of our common experience" (*US,* 189), he does not find it unthinkable that the God whom reason discerns to be personal would communicate with us. From the God of creation he moves to the God of revelation, the God acting in human history. Knox holds that he does so act, but on his terms, not ours; he will not dazzle us into belief:

> But to say that we will not look at any revelation which does not come to us with headlines, so to speak, all across the page, shouting its message at us, compelling attention and forcing conviction on us—that would be presumptuous, seeing what we are. Beggars, after all, cannot be choosers (*US,* 28–29).

God's communications are real, yet subtle; Knox compares them to a game of hide-and-seek (*PS,* 359). Throughout history, God was preparing mankind for his final self-revelation in Christ, shaping man's mind to receive his message as a bird builds a nest for its eggs (*US,* 195).

While it is primarily in Jewish history that this preparation takes place, it is also reflected in the cultural and religious development of the Gentiles. Political events created a milieu in which the Gospel could spread quickly, borne by the Greek language over Roman roads throughout the empire. More than that, "paganism" is in fact the raw material of redeemed human nature:

> The pagan world hunting all the time for the treasure hidden in the field of human history, and always just missing it because they couldn't believe any good thing would come out of Nazareth. Revelation not a desperate drug for humanity at its worst, but a flood lighting of humanity at its best. . . . Read your classics in *that* spirit, and you are like the audience at a Greek play, knowing what was the end of the story when the actors didn't. You will catch a hundred hints of dramatic irony, a hundred overtones of meaning, because you will see the glory that was Greece and the grandeur that was Rome as Act I in the drama of the Incarnation (*OS,* 345).

Focusing on Jewish history as the immediate "seed-ground of revelation", Knox stresses how remarkable this history is. Most amazing is the very survival of the Jews. In terms of language or race, they differed little from their neighbors. Yet we are not surprised to be told that someone is a Jew, where we would marvel to meet a Hittite. The distinguishing characteristic of the Jews, the answer to the riddle of their survival, lies in their religious identity. Their faith also helps us to recognize the heroes of the Old Testament as real people, not "stained-glass figures who always seem to have gone for a walk with a stick in one hand and a thurible in the other" (*US*, 103).

What is central to the Jewish faith? Knox points first to monotheism:

> Isolate in your mind the picture of a little people, assailed and half-infected by all the superstitions of the ancient world . . . yet ever obstinately retaining, after a thousand half-surrenders and tentative apostasies, the conception of a single God, unique in his majesty, controlling the destinies of all nations and all the forces of the created universe. Is there not, in that picture, something infinitely noble, some quality of unexpectedness which almost demands a special Divine revelation to account for it? (*BC*, 66).

This distinctive tradition of worship exists side by side with a distinctive sense of nationality; the God of the Jews is unique, the relation of the Jews to God is also unique. Here is the second central tenet of their faith, the covenant. "The most inclusive of theologies is paradoxically maintained by the most exclusive of peoples" (*BC*, 67).

The history of this covenant relationship leads the Jews not only to look back at the formative events of their past —the Patriarchs, the Exodus, the Monarchy, the Temple, the Exile—but also to look to the future. The fulfillment of God's promise is yet to come, and in the midst of humiliating political defeats the Jewish faith exhibits a third unique quality, a strong eschatological orientation. Nourished by the "tantalizingly obscure visions of the prophets" (*US*, 200), the Jews of the first century were keyed up with an expectation of the Messiah.

Knox acknowledges that the prophets are never easy reading; his aim as a translator was to make them less unintelligible.[2] Later generations face a disadvantage not encoun-

---

[2] Ronald Knox, *Trials of a Translator* (New York: Sheed and Ward, 1949), pp. 32–34.

tered by the prophets' contemporaries: they do not always know where one prophecy ends and another begins, nor what event occasioned the message. But the prophets themselves were somewhat in the dark:

> Everybody knows, even those of us who have lived most unadventurously, what it is to plod on, for miles it seems, eagerly straining your eyes towards the lights that, somehow, mean home. How difficult it is, when you are doing that, to judge distances! In the pitch darkness, it might be a couple of miles to your destination, it might be a few hundred yards—you cannot tell. So it was, I think, with the Hebrew prophets, as they looked forward to the redemption of their people (*PS, 347*).

How aware were the prophets of their prophesying? Knox is of two minds on this question. When talking about the inspiration of the Bible, he emphasizes that the Holy Spirit did not dictate the text; the books of Scripture were produced by ordinary human effort (*CSM,* 148–49). And the prophets expected their contemporaries to understand what they were talking about.[3] On the other hand, when speaking of the prophetic nature of the Old Testament, he holds that the prophets themselves did not understand their own message:

> I don't suppose that Isaias quite knew what he was talking about when he said, "Behold, a Virgin shall conceive and bear a Son". He just felt impelled, somehow, to say that, because that was what the Holy Spirit wanted him to say (*CSM,* 147).

Whatever the source of these "tantalizingly obscure" writings, Knox' main point is that the events of Jesus' life are the key that fits the lock of the Old Testament (*US,* 69). This conviction is rooted in the writings of the New Testament authors and in the teaching of Jesus himself. Jesus

[3] Ibid., 32.

consciously modeled his actions on the Old Testament prophecies, above all on the lesser known ones referring to the Messiah as the Suffering Servant:

> That is what makes the argument from prophecy so splendid, if you know your Old Testament a little; that our Lord is carefully and consciously tracing out the blue-print of prophecy just when it looks as if he were getting it all wrong. Just when we want to pull him up, as St Peter did, and tell him he is going about the thing in the wrong way, he knows his business better than we do, and sees the whole picture of the Messias when we only see part of it (*US*, 204).

One of the principal tasks of the first Christian writers was to prove that the prophecies of the Old Testament find their fulfillment in the life of Jesus. Scriptural references were jealously treasured by the early Church and "turned into a sort of scrap-book; a store-house of evidence to prove the divine mission of Christ" (*PS*, 475). Of all the New Testament authors, Saint Paul is most representative of this desire to interpret the whole sacred history of the Jews in terms of Christ:

> Not a mirage, those old promises, but a mirror for Christian souls. I don't mean that St Paul had to invent all this for himself; our Lord, during those forty days after his Resurrection, went back to Moses (we are told) and the whole line of prophets, interpreting the words used of himself by the Scriptures. All I want to suggest is that St Paul fills in for us the outline which the Gospels have left indistinct; what *did* it mean, in the long run, that providential history of the Jewish people? St Paul can tell us; the Old Testament is a great overture, introducing beforehand all the motifs of the New (*PS*, 497–98).

Christians are so accustomed to the application of Old Testament texts to Christ, especially in the liturgy, that it is difficult for us to isolate these texts from his life. In translating the Old Testament, Knox faced a struggle between his scholarly instincts, which sought to reproduce the exact nuance of the original text, and his pious instincts, which made him want to emphasize the half-conscious foreshadowing of the New Testament in the Old.[4] The Christian reader of the Old Testament is struck with a kind of paradoxical *déjà vu*; each story seems vaguely familiar not because of something that happened earlier, but because of something that was to happen later: "How often a face or a scene arrests us, only because it bears some resemblance to a face or a scene we love! So it is with the Old Testament figures; they borrow their interest from the future."[5]

This reading of the Old Testament with Christian eyes may blind us to what is perhaps the most striking testimony to its prophetic nature: its inherent incompleteness. The drama of the Old Testament is that the great deliverance by God is continually just going to come off but never does.[6] This incompleteness is seen to best advantage when specific texts are put to one side and the whole panorama of Jewish history is contemplated, as Knox does in the following conference.

---

[4] Ibid., 28.

[5] Ronald Knox, *A Retreat for Priests* (London and New York: Sheed and Ward, 1946), p. 176.

[6] Ronald Knox, *The Priestly Life: A Retreat* (New York: Sheed and Ward, 1958), p. 138.

THE MESSIANIC HOPE

Mr Max Beerbohm has an essay somewhere called QUIA IM-
PERFECTUM, in which he comments on the special pathos
attaching to works of art, or pieces of writing, which great
men began, but never lived to finish. And I suppose it would
be a useful way of filling up a pause in the conversation when
a party was going very badly indeed, to put this question to
all the people present: "If you were allowed so to reverse
history that one of the unfinished masterpieces of literature
should be finished, which one would you choose?" Which
would you? Kubla Khan? Hyperion? Weir of Hermiston?
Not, for goodness' sake, the Faery Queen. I know what my
choice would be, unhesitatingly—the great work of apologetic which Pascal planned, of which only a few golden fragments are left to us, known as the "Thoughts" of Pascal.

Consciously or unconsciously, you have been following
Pascal's method in the conferences you have been having this
term. The Greatness of Man and the Littleness of Man are
contrasted in one of his most splendid passages. He argues
from that to the doctrine of the Fall; and then, by-passing
almost contemptuously the traditional proofs of God's existence, he invites his readers, like the Jansenist he (I'm afraid)
was, to fall back on Scripture. He plunges straight into the
history of the Jewish people, and makes his case rest on the
prophecies. I think it's worth noticing that he doesn't do
that just arbitrarily; he insists that the Jews, whatever you
make of them, are a phenomenon unique in history; a phenomenon, you might almost say, not explained by history.
At the back of our minds, of course—and this was specially

Ronald Knox, "The Messianic Hope", unpublished conference typescript,
n.d. Knox Papers, Mells, Somerset.

true of the atheists of Pascal's time—we all like to see the world and the history of the world as a closed circle, not admitting of any interference from outside; we won't have any miracles, we won't even have any providences—everything is explained by common or garden cause and effect. And Pascal corrects this attitude by pointing to the existence of the Jews; "All right," he says, "but what do you make of that?"

And, you know, he had got something there. Of course, the way he tackles it seems rather naïve to our troubled modern minds; not only does he regard the whole of the Pentateuch as obviously accurate history, but he does so on the ground that it was all written by Moses, and Moses wouldn't have been likely to get it wrong—at the back of his mind, you feel, he is bracketing Moses with Julius Caesar. But even people who don't accept the Old Testament as anything like accurate history, even the people who think that Deuteronomy was written about the same time as the poems of Sappho, and the book of Daniel about the same time as the plays of Plautus—even people like that have still to get over somehow, to explain somehow, a great broad historical fact; namely the survival of the Jewish race as a race all through history. I think I have put it, before now, in this way. Supposing you and I were dining at a restaurant, and I said, "Do you see that man at the next table? He's a Hittite", you would say, "Good Lord, is he really? Nonsense, you must be pulling my leg". But if I said, "Do you see that man at the next table? He's a Jew", you would say, "Hush! Of course he is". And yet, you see, the Hittites were a vast empire, far more important than the Jews ever were; and they have left traces of their civilization lying all over the place on brickbats, only—there are no Hittites, no recognizable Hittites, any longer. For some reason, the Jews have survived as a race; and when you look into the reason, you can't account for it by merely ethnological considerations, or by merely linguistic considerations, because neither the stock nor the language of the Jews differed importantly from those of their neighbours. However unwillingly, you have to admit that the Jews survived because they held to certain religious beliefs.

And, for practical purposes, because they held to one particular religious belief—namely, that they were the chosen people of God. You see, it's common enough, if you may trust the people who set up as experts in such matters, for a particular tribe to believe that it enjoys the special favour of its own tribal God. But then, its own tribal God is only one among a whole lot of tribal Gods, so it's the same for everybody. The extraordinary thing about the Jews, as I expect Father Christie was explaining to you last Sunday, is that they believed—came to believe, anyhow—in a God who was king over all the earth, the universal Background of all human reference, who was nevertheless somehow especially the God of the Jews. That is unique, unless you count the attitude of certain Englishmen at the end of last century, and of certain Germans at the beginning of the present century—but they got it all from the Old Testament in any case. And besides, if they believed themselves to be the special favourites of Providence, it was because they were top dog. The Jews have always believed themselves to be God's special favourites when they were under-dog. Always they cling to the belief that they have a message for mankind; did not God say to Abraham, In thy posterity all the nations of the earth shall be blessed? Some day, there will be a general show-down; the times of the Gentiles will have run out, and the day of the Lord will come; a Messiah will appear to deliver his people, and not to deliver them merely, but to lead them to victory.

Humanly speaking, what right had they to expect anything of the sort? Why should they look forward to world-dominion, a nation of farmers and cattle-breeders in a small way on the fringe of the desert? For a short time, under king Solomon, the united kingdom of Israel and Juda did enjoy unexampled prosperity. By a series of judicious conquests and alliances, Israel seems to have controlled the whole of the land-route between the gulf of Akabah and the ports of Phoenicia, and as the wealth of the east flowed into Europe, it left its tolls behind. But it was a commercial, not an imperial greatness that king Solomon enjoyed; and when the kingdom split up after his death, the trade-route was lost, and the prosperity went with it. Yet somehow the legend grew up that the dynasty of king David would produce, one day, a greater monarch than David himself or Solomon had ever been, a world-figure, to put it at the least. How did that happen, while the kings of Juda pursued their inglorious reign over a tiny mountain state? One moment of public deliverance did, perhaps, contribute to this growth of national sentiment, when the army of king Sennacherib melted away at the very gates of Jerusalem, as Isaias had prophesied that it would. But how was it that for the next two centuries, during which Jerusalem was captured and its people were sold into slavery, a succession of prophets continued to foretell, not merely the restoration of Israel's fortunes, but the approach of a day of judgement, when the heathen nations would fall headlong, and a great kingdom, that of the conquering Messiah, would rise on their ruins?

For us Christian people it is unnecessary to follow out these interesting speculations. Because from our own point

of view we can see quite clearly why the Messianic prophecies were made, and what they pointed forward to. They
pointed forward to the Christian dispensation; and the Jews,
not seeing that, are still puzzled. I think it is good for us to
remember that there are a lot of people in the world to whom
the Messianic prophecies mean something, but something
quite unlike what they mean to us. Take a few of the most
familiar prophecies, and try to read them for a moment
through the eyes of a believing Jew who does not accept
Christ. "Behold, a virgin shall conceive, and bear a Son. . .
Unto us a Child is born, unto us a Son is given. . . The
blind see, the deaf hear, the lepers are cleaned. . . Fear not,
daughter of Sion, behold, they King cometh to them, meek
and riding on an ass" and so on. All those prophecies, if
they have not been fulfilled in Jesus Christ, are still await-
ing their fulfilment. No wonder if we and the Jews are at
cross purposes.

All through the first ages of the Church, our attitude
towards the Jews was one of irritable surprise. The "car-
nal" Jews, we called them; not meaning that they were self-
indulgent or anything of that kind, but that they would go
on interpreting the Messianic prophecies in a literal sense,
as if they foreshadowed an earthly conquest and an earthly
kingdom, instead of reading them spiritually. We didn't find
that so very easy ourselves; after the Resurrection, you will
remember, and just before the Ascension, the Apostles ask
our Lord "Dost thou mean to restore the dominion to Israel
here and now?"—meaning, beyond doubt, that they were
still expecting a political show-down of some kind; and this
was the Apostles! But, after Pentecost, when all the dwellers
in Jerusalem had seen the prophecy of Joel fulfilled, God's
spirit poured out on all flesh—surely after that they would
understand? St Paul, I think, obviously regards the blindness

of the Jews as a mere temporary estrangement, a fit of absent-mindedness. And I believe personally that this made it easier for the first Christians to anticipate, as they obviously did, that the Second Coming of Christ was close at hand, probably would happen in their own life-times. They believed, just as Catholic tradition still believes, that God's ancient people would accept Christ before the end came, and surely before long the Jews would see the point! But they didn't; and then, seventy years after Christ, the Romans came and took away their place and nation; the temple lay in ruins, and there was neither priest nor sacrifice nor prophet; and by now the Fathers of the Church were beside themselves with impatience; anybody could see that the literal interpretation of the Messianic prophecies had gone wrong; the Gentiles had come and razed Jerusalem to the ground, and there was no theophany, no deliverance from the clouds! But gradually we came to accept the situation; nothing was going to make the Jews believe in Christ; and by the Middle Ages they had come to be looked upon as something hardly human, a sort of theological freak; it was no good arguing with them.

Looking back over the unhappy centuries, we have no heart to indulge in recriminations. But we still find ourselves wondering, Why was it that the Jews of our Lord's day, most of them, didn't recognize any fulfilment of the Messianic prophecies in him? Can it really be so watertight, our scheme of apologetics, if the argument from prophecy, a traditional feature of it, didn't carry conviction to men who were all keyed up, so it seems, expecting the prophecies to be fulfilled? Mustn't there be a hole in it somewhere? Pascal's answer to that is an interesting one; he points us to a kind of vicious circle. It had been prophesied that the Jews would reject the Christ when he came, and therefore the

Jews had to disbelieve the prophecies; if they had believed
the prophecies, the prophecies wouldn't have been true. I
think that is a little too slick; Pascal often was. I don't know
that you could point to any passage in the Old Testament
where it is foretold, unequivocally, that the Messiah will
be rejected by his own people. But all the same it's not far
off the mark. The trouble about the Jews, as our Lord himself pointed out, was that they stoned the prophets when
they were alive, and built magnificent tombs to them when
they were dead. They had that conservative habit of mind
which misses its opportunities because its oracles are those
of yesterday. That is, surely, what he means when he tells the
Pharisees, "Your fathers stoned the prophets, and you build
their tombs; by which you make it clear that you are your
fathers' children". He means that the conservative habit of
mind which canonizes the last prophet but one is the same
habit of mind which shuts its ears against the prophet of the
day. Experience ought to have taught them the importance
of recognizing the true prophet when he came; that was the
lesson the Jews might have learnt, and didn't.

At the same time, although it's not quite clear whether
they ought to have foreseen that they were going to reject
the Messiah, it is quite clear they ought to have foreseen
that he would be rejected; that he would be a Man, pas-
sible and suffering; that he would be put to death for the
sins of his people. If you doubt that, you have only to go
home and read the 53rd chapter of Isaias. Controversy still
rages about those later chapters of Isaias' prophecy; about
who it was the prophet meant, in the first instance, when
he wrote about "the just one, my servant". But the words
of that chapter, familiar to us from a hundred quotations,
"All the while it was for our sins he was wounded, it was
guilt of ours crushed him down; on him the punishment fell

that brought us peace, by his bruises we were healed," and so on—don't tell me that doesn't belong to the corpus of Messianic prophecy. Yet somehow the Jews seem to have overlooked it, seem to have hushed it up. It's very interesting to notice what they are represented as saying about the Christ in the 12th chapter of St John. Our Lord has just told them, "If only I am lifted up from the earth, I will attract all men to myself"; and their comment is, "We have been told, out of the law, that Christ is to remain undisturbed for ever; what dost thou mean by saying that the Son of Man must be lifted up?" They think of the Christ, you see, as inaugurating a reign of undisturbed peace, a millennium; and the word "lifted up" suggests to them—it was meant to suggest to them—being killed, being removed from the earth. They couldn't reconcile the two ideas; you see, they hadn't been reading their fifty-third chapter of Isaias.

Well, you object, perhaps it wasn't a very well-known chapter; it occurs right at the end of the book, and the casual reader wouldn't be likely to come across it. All right, look on a few pages; turn up the eighth chapter of the Acts. St Philip the deacon is walking along the great road that led southwards from Samaria; a chariot passes him, going the same way, and he thumbs a lift. The owner is a rather important person, a Ras from Abyssinia, a proselyte to the Jewish religion. He is reading the Bible to himself, and badly wanting the one-volume commentary; he can't make head or tail of it. "The passage of scripture which he was reading was this; He was led away like a sheep to be slaughtered; like a lamb that is dumb before its shearer, he would not open his mouth. His life is being cut off from the earth. . . . Tell me, about whom does the prophet say this? Himself, or some other man?" Yes, he was reading the fifty-third chapter of Isaias, and he was asking himself the question the Jews ought to have been asking themselves in our Lord's lifetime. The very word, "his life is being *cut off*" is the same word which puzzled the Jews so much when our Lord used it, "lifted up" from the earth. Oh, yes the Jews ought to have known.

The argument from prophecy, as Pascal saw, is a perfectly good argument, and we mustn't be ashamed of using it just because the Jews, who had the key in their hands, couldn't unlock the door—it's easy to miss the thing that matters, if your mind is preoccupied with something else. But I think there is just this about the argument from prophecy which sometimes gives us pause; it seems to belong to an older period of religious controversy. A period, I mean, when people spent their time flinging texts at one another, with very little regard to the context; when you could tell Galileo that he was no scientist, because he'd only got to read the psalms to find out that the earth didn't move. We are always being confronted with a verse here, a section there, which does seem rather a coincidence in view of what happened afterwards, but still, was it necessarily more than a coincidence? And, worse still, these isolated Messianic texts don't always bear—at least, not to the satisfaction of the scholars—the interpretation which piety has put on them. "A virgin shall conceive, and bear a son"—yes, but the word doesn't necessarily mean more than a marriageable woman. In the posterity of Abraham all mankind shall be blessed—yes, but it may only mean that all mankind will regard Abraham's posterity as uncommonly lucky. It's a cheeseparing process, surely, this business of proving the Christian religion from prophecy?

I think there's a good deal in that. The text-books of theology are all too accurately described as text-books: and in the New Testament itself you get tired of St Paul's manipu-

lation of a phrase here, a phrase there—he was a Jew arguing with Jews, and it was the Jewish instinct to regard the
Law as a series of jots and tittles. What you want to do—I
wish Catholics did it oftener—is to read the Old Testament
as a whole; to see what a dull piece of archaeology it is, if
it has no meaning beyond itself, how it all comes alive if
you read it with the New Testament as your book-marker.
The promises made to the patriarchs, how hopelessly over-
done they seem, if they only refer to the fortunes of one no-
mad tribe! The flight from Egypt, how interminably dwelt
on and emphasized, if it was a mere national deliverance,
and not the forecast of some greater deliverance to come!
The tabernacle and its fittings, the Jewish priesthood and
its sacrifices, what was the sense of localizing and nation-
alizing the God of heaven and earth, unless perhaps these
were only types and shadows, destined to grow dim in the
full light of day? King David and his dynasty, such a long
series of ineffective satellite kings, where lies the interest of
them, unless they are only the beginning of a story? And
then the prophets, so crabbed and incomprehensible, what
patience can you have with them until you see that they
were big with a message which they had no language to express? *Can* that be *all*? QUIA IMPERFECTUM—in all literature,
there is nothing so incomplete as the Old Testament, unless
it found its completion in the New.

12

"WHAT IT WAS THAT MET THE GAZE OF THE APOSTLES": THE PERSON OF JESUS

When treating the core of Christian faith, the identity and mission of Jesus of Nazareth, Knox encourages his apologist to

> prove the divineness of Our Lord's mission, not by presenting us with a series of logical dilemmas, but by trying to reconstruct the picture of Our Lord Himself, what it was that met the gaze of the Apostles, and the touch of their hands (*PGNA*, 16).

Knox himself had tried both approaches. One of the criticisms leveled against him by Arnold Lunn in *Roman Converts* concerned his preference for "the queer, logic-chopping legalistic interpretation" of Jesus:

> The gospels are full of pictures. Knox's sermons are full of party points. Knox's Jesus never comes to life. His secret, his simplicity, the magic of his words, an alchemy which transformed all values and changed the world, finds no place in Knox's scheme.[1]

Yet such "logical dilemmas" are only a small part of the picture. In many of his sermons, Knox touches the hearts of

---

[1] Arnold Lunn, *Roman Converts* (London: Chapman and Hall, 1924), p. 179.

his listeners as profoundly as any of the great preachers of the twentieth century; these "pictures of Our Lord Himself" are among Knox' most effective apologetical writings. The first part of this chapter will offer a summary of his logical argumentation for the divine identity of Jesus as presented in *The Belief of Catholics*, the second part will explore the fuller apologetic found in his other writings.

Sifting the Evidence: Who Is Jesus?

Did Jesus of Nazareth claim to be God? Explicitly, Knox responds, no. Yet there is much evidence that Jesus considered himself divine. Indirectly, two objections to such a claim in fact argue for Jesus' divine self-identity: his injunctions for silence about his identity and his insistence on his humanity. Concerning the former, the secrecy regarding his identity was due to a need to reshape the popular understanding of the Messiah; a premature assertion of his claim would have led "to a crown in Galilee, a shower of stones in Judea" (*BC,* 86). In regard to the latter point, Knox believes that on two occasions Jesus deliberately asserted the fact of his humanity: telling his disciples about his Temptation at the outset of his ministry and sharing with them his experience of the Agony in the garden before his arrest. Why should he underscore his humanity, unless he was conscious that he was more than human?

Knox introduces three pieces of more direct evidence: (1) Jesus identified himself with the Son of Man, awaited by the Jews as deliverer and judge; (2) in speaking about God, he implied a unique sense of Sonship, as when he spoke of "my Father" and "your Father" but never of "our Father"; (3) he proposed to perform miracles in his own name.

As a final piece of evidence, Knox considers the trial of Jesus and his affirmative response to the high priest's question, "Art thou the Christ, the Son of the Blessed God?" That the question was framed in such a way as to invoke a divine claim may be seen by the cry of "blasphemy" that greeted Jesus' response.

The force of the arguments presented in this chapter "Our Lord's Claim Stated", can best be realized according to Knox if the reader asks himself, "If Jesus did not claim to be God, what did he claim to be?"

> Is it credible that he did what he did, said what he said, hinted what he hinted, kept silence when he kept silence, and finally answered the challenge of Caiphas without a word of qualification, of explanation, or of self-defense, if all the time he belonged, and was conscious of belonging, to any order of Being less than Divine? Where was the need of all this mystery, these veiled allusions, these injunctions of silence, if they only served to foster a false impression, which a couple of sentences would have cleared up? (*BC,* 91).

In his next chapter, "Our Lord's Claim Justified", Knox argues that Christ's claim to be divine can be justified. Since the Catholic Church is challenging the human intellect to a duel on this critical point, Knox observes the courtesy of allowing his reader a choice of weapons. Presuming that such a choice may involve a rejection of miracles, he begins by temporarily dismissing the whole notion of the miraculous from the life of Jesus and asking how we can judge his career.

If Jesus was not God, yet claimed to be, he must either have been an impostor or the victim of a delusion. An impostor? Knox points out that it is impossible to find a motive for any pretense on Jesus' part, since he pointedly disassociated himself from political power, wealth, or the adulation of the crowds. Was Jesus then insane? Certainly there have been charismatic religious leaders who were deluded; the charge cannot be ruled out of court with a wave of the hand. Knox argues that "the suggestion of madness is inconsistent with the breadth of vision and the originality of thought (to put it at its lowest) which are displayed by our Lord's teaching" (*BC, 95*). Jesus is recognized as one of the greatest religious geniuses of history, even by those outside the Christian religion. This would be inconsistent with insanity:

> Lunacy does not fail to give itself away. As well expect a motor-car to find its way through crowded traffic without a driver, as a mind that is unbalanced to commit itself to literary expression without being guilty of extravagances that betray it (*BC, 96*).

This is as far as Knox can advance an inquiry into the identity of Jesus from which the miraculous element is barred.

He introduces his second approach by recalling that God has revealed himself in creation as All-Righteous, All-Wise, and All-Powerful. This threefold revelation is mirrored in the life of Jesus: God's Goodness is seen in his words and actions, God's Wisdom is reflected in the fulfillment of the Old Testament prophecies, and God's Power is found in Jesus' miracles.

Concerning the miracles, Knox begins by asserting that in the first century, a "blaze of credulity" flared up; not only "ignorant peasants" but also rich people like Barnabas, educated ones like Paul, physicians like Luke were "swept away on this odd stream of belief in miracle" (*BC, 101*). Odd, because for Jews and pagans alike, the miraculous was associated with antiquity; belief in miracles "began again" in the first century. From this, Knox concludes:

> The least that can reasonably be said is that our Lord's lifetime was accompanied by certain events which—ignorantly,

perhaps; stupidly, perhaps—people took to be supernatural events. You have a right to your own opinion, but do not deny that the strange events happened; that notion fails to account for this sudden outburst (if you will) of credulity which began in the first century and has continued ever since in the Christian Church (*BC,* 101).

For economy of space, Knox limits himself to a consideration of one miracle, while recognizing that it hardly falls into line with the rest: the Resurrection. He begins with two "plain facts": Jesus expected to rise from the dead, and his tomb was found empty on Easter morning. The empty tomb then provides his point of departure. The only plausible "natural" explanations to account for it are that Jesus did not really die on the Cross, or that his disciples secretly carried off his corpse. If the former were the case, we would have to hold that Jesus intentionally deluded posterity into the belief that he died and rose again. Can that be reconciled with the impression we have formed of his character from his teaching and life? If the second explanation were true, we would have to believe that the disciples deliberately preached a Gospel they knew to be a hoax. Can that be reconciled with the transformation of their behavior between the times of Jesus' arrest and Pentecost?

Then there are also the Resurrection appearances to account for. The narratives of these are preserved in fragmentary and confused form, which testifies to their authenticity—they have not been doctored. That these appearances were only visions would contradict the accounts indicating that the risen Lord could be touched, the evidence of the empty tomb, and the testimony of the first Christians that these encounters were unlike later "visions". Knox concludes his defense of the miracle of the Resurrection by asking, "And do we still find the story of the Resurrection fabulous? Shall we not rather reserve the epithet for the theories which scholarship has invented to explain it away?" (*BC,* 107).

In *The Belief of Catholics*, Knox attempts to meet the unbeliever on his own ground. He does not want to be guilty of saying to the would-be convert, "Unfortunately there is something of a gap in the argument here; let us hasten to fill it up with the putty of sentiment" (*PGNA,* 43).

Even so, after reviewing the arguments Knox puts forward, it is possible to counter the question concluding his story of the Resurrection with another, which much later in life he puts to his imaginary apologist:

> On paper . . . your arguments are beautifully convincing; but, tell me, has any human being ever been converted to God in that way? Can you point to a single instance, in history or among your own acquaintance, where a man has been led on, unwillingly, by sheer force of argument, to a position in which mere intellectual candour forced him to make the surrender of his soul? (*PGNA,* 36).

"The Picture of Our Lord Himself"

It would be unfair to Ronald Knox to confine a study of his apologetics concerning Christ to the forensic approach he adopts in *The Belief of Catholics*. In many of his sermons and retreats, he lays before his hearers "what it was that met the gaze of the Apostles, and the touch of their hands". The second part of this chapter will fill in Knox' apologetic picture of Jesus by exploring this material.

The Divinity of Christ

In one of his early Oxford conferences, Knox covers much of the same ground concerning Jesus' claim as he did in

The Belief of Catholics.[2] He presents examples of statements made by Jesus that reflect his unique relationship with the Father. One of these takes on added significance because it tells not only of Jesus' relation to the Father but also of his relation to his disciples: "My Father has entrusted everything into my hands; none knows the Son truly except the Father, and none knows the Father truly except the Son, and those to whom it is the Son's good pleasure to reveal him" (Mt 11:27). There is a mutual knowledge between the Father and the Son, which the Son is in a position to share with his earthly friends. He comes to bring a revelation about God that none but he could know.

This passage finds an echo later in Matthew, when Peter makes his confession that Jesus is the Messiah and is told in response, "Blessed art thou, Simon son of Jona; it is not flesh and blood, it is my Father in heaven that has revealed this to thee" (Mt 16:17). Just as Jesus reveals the Father to his disciples, so they learn of Jesus' identity from the Father. The disciples are the witnesses of this mutual revelation. In fact, Knox bases his own belief in the divinity of Jesus not on logical arguments but on the testimony of the Apostles:

> Now, if the Apostles didn't believe in our Lord's Divinity, why on earth should I? That he was an accredited Medium of a divine revelation, I believe on merely historical grounds; that he was personally God is a view upon which (at least) I could have no certainty, if it were not part of a continuous tradition handed down by the Apostles themselves (*Dif,* 232).

There is another testimony to the divinity of Jesus that paradoxically stands in opposition to Knox' approach in *The Belief of Catholics*. In that book, he had drawn attention to the striking credentials of Jesus: the impact of his teaching, the warrant of his miracles, the correlation between the events

[2] Ronald Knox, "The Claim", in *US,* 33–39.

of his life and the prophecies of the Old Testament. In a later sermon, he finds evidence of his divinity in the ordinariness of Jesus' life:

> He came, and the world missed the portents of his coming. The stars could not keep the secret, they blurted it out to the wise men, their cronies; the angels could not keep the secret, they sang it to the shepherds over the fields of Bethlehem. But the world, the world of fashion and intelligence, was looking the other way. What, after all, was there for it to see? A baby, crying at its mother's breast; a boy working in a carpenter's shop; a street-corner orator, producing a nine-days wonder among the fisher-folk at Capharnaum; a discredited popular leader, ignominiously put to death; a corpse lying in a tomb—and this was God! He rose again, but in doing so he showed himself to none but a handful of chosen witnesses; the world looked to find him, and he was gone. Would you know that Jesus Christ is divine? Then see how he imitates, in his humanity, the reticence of the God who created the world and left it to forget him, the God who rules the world, yet rules it imperceptibly; and recognize, in the masterpiece of the Incarnation, the touch of the same artist's brush (*PS,* 326–27).

The Humanity of Christ

It is in his humanity that Jesus reveals the Father to us. When addressing unbelievers, Knox is concerned to defend the divinity of Christ; when speaking to Catholics, he stresses his humanity. Christians accustomed to adoring the divine Jesus need to be reminded that

> close to God, with a closeness you and I cannot imagine, reigns eternally one who is a man of our own flesh and blood, who knows what it feels like to suffer and be tempted, who is proud of us because we belong to him, who wants us to

follow him to heaven and be near him; near, through him, to his heavenly Father (*CSM,* 133).

When the Church proclaims that God became Man, "she is not guilty of a metaphor or a piece of pulpit rhetoric" (*US,* 102). Through the Incarnation, the goodness of God has been translated into human terms; revelation has been tailored to our needs:

> To be intelligible to us at all, the things of eternity must be thrown on the screen of time. A life, a life which involved action, perhaps even a life which involved suffering, was necessary if we were to have a revelation made to us. If Einstein were to teach schoolboys geometry, he would need a blackboard; but that is the schoolboys' fault, not Einstein's (*Dif,* 156).

Since this is the case, then all of Jesus' life must be seen as a revelation of the Father, and the most ordinary human experiences are communications of God. Jesus shared our emotions of anger, wonder, sorrow, and joy, the last constituting for Knox the most outstanding proof of his humanity (*PS,* 189). The Evangelists tell us that God became Man, but that is not all:

> They tell me more than that; how God made Man was God made a Boy, who grew in wisdom with the years; how he underwent baptism, the baptism which was ordained for the remission of sins; how he was tempted by the devil; how he was surprised, and asked questions; how he chose a scoundrel to be one of his most intimate friends; how he wept with disappointment over the infidelity of Jerusalem; how he shrank from the near approach of death; how he complained aloud, on his Cross, that God had forsaken him. And as paradox after paradox comes out, the theologians sit there making it all right, and saying, "Here we distinguish; in one sense yes, and in another sense no", but the Evangelists just go on with

their story; "we don't know about that" they explain; "all we know is that this is what happened."[3]

As one who has shared our common experience, Jesus offers us a human friendship. True, this friendship can seem unreal at times, or impersonal; it is ordinarily hidden for us under sacramental veils. But that is also the case with our other friendships, which communicate themselves under the veil of handwriting or a particular tone of voice (*PS*, 280). This invitation to friendship is unique: "You will find nothing like it in any other religion; you may take Mahomet for your prophet, Buddha for your teacher—only Jesus invites you to be his friend" (*PS*, 371).

The Teaching of Christ

Jesus stands alone among great religious figures not only because of his invitation to friendship but also because of his teaching. This uniqueness is blurred because people have constructed an image of Jesus as a great spiritual master with "cut-and-paste" techniques. This image is composed of general moral aphorisms, but excludes striking statements Jesus made about himself:

> Our Lord didn't come to give us a set of helpful quotations to print in calendars. He came to tell us about himself. Did Confucius ever say, "All power is given to me in heaven and in earth"? Did Mahomet ever say, "No one cometh to the Father but by me"? Did Buddha ever say, "Whoever confesseth me before men, the same will I confess before my Father who is in heaven"? (*US*, 227).

[3] Ronald Knox, "The New Testament Record", unpublished conference typescript, 1952, Knox Papers, Mells, Somerset, pp. 8–9; see pp. 202–11 of this book.

It is true that Christ was a great moral teacher who has altered the standards of behavior that people honor. His instruction has led to the breakdown of many social barriers and enriched personal virtues with new meaning. Knox gives three examples of the latter: humility, which formerly meant only "lowness, baseness, insignificance" until the word came to stand for a virtue when used by Christian authors; charity, limited in its original meaning to affection for friends and family until Jesus taught that it is also owed to strangers; and purity, a matter of externals until Jesus showed that purity has its root in the heart (*PS,* 366–67). However, although Jesus was a great moral teacher, Knox points out that it is unhistorical to see him as a spiritual master who was thought by later ages to have risen from the dead: "The message which electrified the world of the first century was not 'Love your enemies,' but 'He is risen'."[4]

The whole Christian understanding of life—morality, sacraments, evangelical counsels—rests on the teaching of Jesus, but this in turn is established on his divine identity. As far back as *Some Loose Stones,* Knox stressed the unique teaching authority of Jesus; to question it is to challenge the most basic elements of Christianity:

> "This is my Body, This is my Blood"; may not that be a strange delusion, an empty boast? "Whoso marrieth one that is divorced committeth adultery"; wasn't that perhaps a fad? A little piece of pardonable bigotry? "Go ye into all the world, and preach the Gospel to every creature"; wasn't that unduly sanguine? . . . "Ye cannot serve God and Mammon"— otherworldliness, out of harmony with the spirit of the twentieth century. . . . That is Christianity without the Ipse Dixit of our Saviour; and who shall prove the validity of that Ipse

[4] Ronald Knox, *Caliban in Grub Street* (London: Sheed and Ward: 1930), p. 113.

Dixit, if Jesus of Nazareth laboured under a lifelong illusion?
(*SLS,* 123–24).

In his parables, Jesus does not mouth a string of moral maxims. He speaks of how God's grace follows us everywhere, seeking out, healing, perfecting; sin, rejection, forgiveness are themes of a great drama and contain a challenge. In response, we, like his first listeners, "if we will only listen, must either crucify or adore" (*PS,* 145).

The core of Jesus' moral teaching is a call to freedom. The fulfillment of the law does not mean more commandments; it means commandments of a different kind (*PS,* 56). A principle of active charity supersedes the need for commandments. Knox contrasts the person who only wants to keep the Commandments, to serve God without loving him, with the person who has mastered the Sermon on the Mount and rests in the love of Christ:

> Think of a ship outside the harbour at anchor. See how winds and tides drive it to and fro; how it is continually tugging at the chains that moor it. The strain is never eased for long; one faulty link, and at any moment the ship may drive out to sea. That is like a soul that is only moored by the Ten Commandments. Winds and tides of passion sweep it to and fro. . . . And now think of a ship riding at anchor in harbour. She is moored, yes, sure enough; but how lightly she tugs at her moorings! They have hardly any work to do, the strain is so slight. That is just an image of the soul that rides on the love of Jesus Christ (*PS,* 60).

For Knox, Jesus' teaching can never be separated from his person. His is a double authority: as the Son of God, he commands with full divine power; as the teacher who is "meek and humble of heart", he attracts by his example. Through his ministry, his availability, his patience, and gentleness, Jesus lived the New Law he preached. But he also did so through his miracles, which cannot simply be set aside.

The Miracles of Christ

In *The Belief of Catholics*, Knox approached the identity of Jesus along two avenues, according to whether the reader accepts or rejects the possibility of miracles. In a pamphlet written for the Catholic Truth Society in the same year, he explores the question of the miraculous more fully.[5]

When discussing the possibility of the miraculous, the Christian has to do battle on two fronts. On the one hand, there are people who maintain that miracles can never happen; on the other, those who hold that they are always happening. In the first camp, Knox locates Deists, who conceive of God as separated from creation once he has set it in motion, and Pantheists, for whom God is so enmeshed in creation that he cannot exempt himself from its laws.

To these understandings of God, Knox opposes the Christian view that God not only created but sustains the world. It is his will that is at the root of all scientific causality; the daily functioning of creation is itself a miracle:

> You are puzzled by miracles? I tell you, if you could only recognize the necessity of God's action in the world, the fall of a sparrow to the ground would be ten thousand times more staggering to your poor, finite imagination. It is a thing to make you dream at night, and wake gasping with the wonder of it.[6]

The God who is the source of the laws of nature can also express his will by suspending those laws. But granted that

[5] Ronald Knox, *Miracles* (London: Catholic Truth Society, 1927).
[6] Ibid., p. 7.

God *can* do miracles, why would he? Knox gives two reasons. First, God performs miracles because we need reminders of him:

> So a great artist might trust that the skilfulness of his own painting would be enough warrant of its genuineness; and yet —men are so hesitating, so hard to please! At the last moment he scrawls his PINXIT in the corner. Miracles are God's signature, appended to His masterpiece of creation, not because they ought to be needed, but because they are needed.[7]

Secondly, God performs miracles to draw our attention not to himself but to one of his servants; miracles are signs of accreditation for his authorized messengers.

This raises the question of the second approach to miracles, which holds that they are not only possible, but common. They are found in all religions and in no religion. The Spiritualist can speak of phenomena for which science is unable to account; the Christian Scientist testifies that miraculous healings are not only possible, that in fact they happen every day. Given the universality of the miraculous, how can it be claimed as a sign of accreditation by any one body or person?

The Christian understanding of miracles differs from this approach in two ways. The Christian *hopes* for a miracle; the Spiritualist and the Christian Scientist *expect* one. For the Christian, God grants supernatural favors with sovereign freedom: they are not phenomena that can be regularly produced. Secondly, Christian miracles are always experienced in a context that demands that they be given a spiritual interpretation. The witness of power and moral witness are inseparable, above all in the miracles of Jesus (*US,* 217–19).

[7] Ibid., p. 10.

Concerning the Gospel miracles, Knox makes several observations. First, he maintains that it is impossible to purge the miraculous element from the Gospels. Miracle "haunts the story at every turn" (*US,* 219) and, more importantly, suits the narrative. If in fact the appearance of Christ is the unique self-revelation of God, it is fitting that the supernatural should be part of the atmosphere. The reaction of the natural world to this invasion by the supernatural expresses itself in miracle:

> The diseases, the leprosy, the deafness, the blindness, the disfigured and distorted limbs, the paralysis—they are all part of the world's darkness; and when the light shines, the darkness yields to it; this positive thing overawes our negatives; the sick get well, the blind see, and so on. It is miracle, yes, in the natural order; and yet if you think what the supernatural is, the wonder would be if these strange results didn't follow, when the supernatural breaks in upon us as it did at the Incarnation (*US,* 221).

Further, the miracles of Jesus testify to his divinity:

> Put Raphael down at a street-corner as a pavement-artist, what proof can he give of his identity but to paint like Raphael? Bring God down to earth, what proof can He give of His Godhead but to command the elements like God?[8]

But they testify as well to his humanity; when Jesus says he is moved with pity for the crowd, he proclaims his solidarity with mankind in its experience of revulsion in the presence of suffering (*PS,* 288).

The miracles of Jesus are an essential part of the Gospel; they bear witness to his power and to his mercy. But they are also inseparable from his teaching. Knox compares Jesus performing a miracle to a person moving knives and salt-cellars

[8] Knox, *Miracles,* p. 17.

about on a table to illustrate a story; the miracles illustrate the lessons Jesus teaches (*US*, 221). They are not done to dazzle us, but to enlighten us; they should be seen as both historical fact and theological meaning. This was how the early Church understood the miracles, and such an appreciation is enshrined in the Gospel accounts. The fact—be it the multiplication of the loaves and fishes, or the healing of the blind man at the pool of Siloe, of the Resurrection itself —had to be interpreted in terms of its meaning for those who were not present at the event. Christ's teaching and his miracles form the warp and woof of the same fabric:

> We mustn't let people think of our Lord's miracles as if they were a set of theatrical performances, thrown out by a well-known preacher in order to draw attention to himself. They are part of his message; a sign-language between heaven and earth, pictures of eternity cast on the screen of time. . . . Say, if you will, that his miracles come to us bathed in the light of his teaching. Or say, if you will, that his teaching comes to us pegged down to reality—supernatural reality—by his miracles. But you must examine his life as a whole, as a unity, not broken up into strands (*US*, 223).

The Passion and Death of Christ

The teaching, ministry, and miracles of Jesus constitute only one half of any Gospel narrative; the other half comprises the reactions to Jesus. In his sermons, Knox portrays the varying responses to Jesus found in the Gospels, inviting his hearers to reflect on their own reaction to him. The challenge of Jesus is offered most dramatically in his death. In the Cross, the whole teaching and mission of Christ finds its most intense expression. It is an event allowing no innocent bystanders:

There was no spectator at the death on Calvary, however casual, however insignificant, that did not carry away in his heart the seed of life or of death. There has been and will be no human creature who, when the last sheaf is bound and the last load garnered, will not be found to have accepted or refused the seed of life, and in accepting or refusing it signed the warrant of his own eternal destiny (*PS*, 150).

In a series of sermons preached in Lent, 1928, Knox uses the parable of the sower and the seed to reflect on "the harvest of the Cross".[9] Various characters of the Passion are presented and their diverse reactions are linked with modern responses to Christ.

There is first the seed that fell by the wayside, which represents those whose minds and hearts are hardened so that they will not even hear the invitation of Christ. Here are found Pilate, the soldiers, the impenitent thief, who stand for an attitude of indifference among believers and unbelievers alike. Prejudice, conventionality, or insensibility prevent the seed of the Gospel from ever taking root: "Hard hearts, not broken hearts, are the world's tragedy" (*US*, 334).

The seed that fell on stony ground is an image of those who have been attracted by Jesus but whose faith is too shallow to withstand the withering sun of the Cross. Here are the Galilean followers ("cradle Catholics"), Jews of Judea (converts), and Herod ("cultured dabblers" in matters of religion), all attracted by Jesus for a time. But when following Jesus is no longer fashionable, no longer carries the promise of earthly reward, the plant withers.

Next comes the seed that fell among thorns, those in whom the word of Christ has taken root only to be choked

[9] "The Harvest of the Cross" was first published in Ronald Knox, *The Mystery of the Kingdom* (London: Sheed and Ward, 1928); reprinted in *PS*, 149–80.

by riches, pleasures, other cares. Here Knox locates Judas and also alludes to the figure of Demas, who "has fallen in love with this present world; he has deserted me, and gone to Thessalonica" (2 Tim 4:9). For persons such as these, the Gospel message has taken root but cannot overcome competing attractions.

From the various types in whom the Cross produces no harvest, Knox turns to those in whom it bears fruit. Even here there is variety. The seed that bore fruit thirtyfold represents those who have come to know their own weakness by their abandonment of Christ and who now rely on him all the more. Here we find the disciples after their desertion, especially the repentant Peter, whose "tears were the rain that made the good seed spring up thirtyfold" (*PS*, 167).

Three disciples are singled out as those who have borne fruit sixtyfold and a hundredfold: Mary Magdalen, John, and Our Lady. They are the faithful watchers by the Cross; each depicts the contemplative Christian in a distinctive way. For Mary Magdalen, the crucifixion was not a test of character but an opportunity for love. If she is the mourner, John is the learner, the witness who will pass on to others the meaning of the event. Our Lady is the one who unites her will completely with her Son's; her participation is com-passion in the truest sense of the word.

Accordingly, Magdalen is a type of our affections, John of our minds, Mary of our wills. Knox invites us to recognize in them how the crucified Jesus speaks to these three faculties in each of us. In his Passion, Christ quickens our affections, so often denigrated but so important for our spiritual life. He also answers the questions of our intellect concerning suffering and pain; not completely, of course, but with a sense that they can have value when united with his.

Finally, he confirms the purpose of our wills, the goal of knowing and loving the Crucified:

> And if we can learn from Mary something of the secret by which at that dark hour she made her will all his, it will be no transient upheaval of the emotions, no mere enlargement of the horizon of our speculative intellect, but a true determination of the will to action and endurance that we shall carry away with us as we turn to go down the hill, back into the dust of the city and the world that has crucified its God (*PS,* 177).

The problem of human suffering takes on added mystery when it is contemplated in Christ crucified: the culmination of a life devoted to combatting suffering in others is found in the Cross. Conventional explanations of suffering—such as that it is a punishment for wrongdoing or an opportunity to perfect one's character or prove a disinterested love for God—do not apply in the case of the sinless Son of God on Calvary. Rather than shedding light on the question of suffering, it appears that the Cross only accents the absurdity of ever understanding the mystery.

Jesus' Passion does not offer an explanation unraveling the problem of pain; it does give an inspiration that enables us to accept it. An important avenue of approach in this regard is the doctrine of the atonement. As early as *Some Loose Stones*, Knox defended the idea that the general apostasy of mankind called for death and that only the sacrifice of the Sinless One could be an equivalent compensation (*SLS,* 173). In effecting this reconciliation, the innocent suffers on behalf of the guilty. Jesus reveals a new dimension to the human intuition that suffering is linked somehow to sin: suffering can be a means of expiating for the sins of others.

By uniting our sufferings with those of Christ, we make them an instrument of reconciliation:

> If we have learned in all our adversities, in sickness, in sorrow, in bereavement, in anxiety, in desolation, yes, even in doubts and scruples, to unite ourselves with his Passion, ours is the pain that heals: the more to suffer, the more to offer, that is the first principle of the Christian medicine (*PS*, 86).

"The more to suffer, the more to offer" is bitter medicine; our natural instinct is to avoid pain. But generosity in suffering marks the Passion of Jesus, who does not aim at suffering as little as possible: "The splendid profusion of the Precious Blood shall be the charter of his kingdom and the badge of his service" (*US*, 369). This generosity takes a curious form: Jesus does not keep his sufferings to himself but shares them with his friends. The disciples in the garden of Gethsemane and at the foot of the Cross are present because Jesus wants them (and us) to share in his work of redemption by sharing in his pain. But he has first shared in our suffering:

> He let them nail him to the Cross, those feet which tired on the roads of Galilee idle now, that hand which had often reversed our human tragedies motionless. It was as if he wanted us to see that the greatest act of all his life was what he did when he seemed powerless to do anything. Tied hand and foot, he could still pardon, and absolve, and love. . . . To let ourselves suffer, only because it is his will; to let ourselves suffer, perhaps as he did, from the neglect and the cruelty and the contempt of our fellow men—that is the chief, and perhaps the hardest thing he asks of us. But he does ask it of us (*PS*, 273).

Suffering remains a mystery, with Jesus adding paradox to mystery. Throughout his life, he waged a campaign against suffering in others and banished pain wherever he encountered it; in his own life, he welcomed it as his vocation. His most illustrious followers, the saints, have dedicated their lives to alleviating suffering—founding hospitals, orphanages, soup-kitchens, and schools—and have at the same time recognized pain in their own lives as a mark of special favor from God. Attempting to account for this ambiguity, Knox uses the following image with the schoolgirls at Aldenham:

> If you look at an electric light bulb when it isn't burning, you will see nothing inside but a rather uninteresting-looking bit of wire; and you might be tempted to say to yourself, "I don't see how anybody's going to get light out of that." But, once you switch the current on, that piece of wire does give light, because the electricity transmutes it into a glowing mass. So it is with suffering in human lives; an evil thing in itself, it becomes a good thing when it is transmuted, by the love of God, into a glowing focus of charity (*CSM,* 75–76).

Jesus not only suffered, he died. By accepting even death, Christ experienced fully what it means to be human. In so doing, he has given us encouragement in the face of death:

> I think he wanted to fortify our imaginations against the uncomfortable feeling we all have when we go to a funeral, and the coffin is smothered in earth. . . . When you were very small, and had to take medicine, did your mother ever take a sip first, just so as to assure you that everything was all right? That is what Jesus Christ did, when he was buried for us (*CSM,* 103).

The Resurrection of Christ

In *The Belief of Catholics*, Ronald Knox presents the Resurrection as the greatest of Christ's miracles, the proof that his divine claim was justified. But it is far more than this; in *The Creed in Slow Motion*, Knox writes that the Resurrection constitutes not only a proof but also a hope and a challenge (*CSM,* 116).

In some of his Easter sermons, Knox employs variations on the approach he took in *The Belief of Catholics*: the Gospel accounts are presented as evidence, the congregation constituting the jury.[10] In these talks, he emphasizes the reliability of the Easter narratives in several ways. For example, he argues that the confused nature of the accounts of Easter day actually testifies to their authenticity:

> The evidence on these points of detail is not exactly clear. True evidence very seldom is. Bribe a handful of soldiers, and they will spread the same lie all over Jerusalem. Take three women to the tomb, none of them expecting to find anything unusual, and you will have to piece the story together for yourself (*PS,* 387).

He also uses the figure of Thomas to point out that the witnesses to the Resurrection were not credulous. This apostle was

> one of those people who will always ask the inconvenient question. One of those hard-headed, you might almost say bullet-headed, people who give so much trouble on juries and on committees of every sort by refusing to take the majority view until they, personally, are satisfied (*PS,* 402).

As to the explanation that the appearances of the risen Christ were a hallucination, Knox points out that they were just the opposite. The disciples frequently did not recognize the risen Lord. A hallucination causes us to mistake a

---

[10] Ronald Knox, "Early in the Morning", in *US,* 39; and "The Guarded Tomb", in *PS,* 386.

stranger for a friend; they mistook their friend for a stranger (*PS,* 389).

Finally, Knox strengthens his argument by connecting the evidence of the empty tomb and the accounts of Easter day with other data:

> The events I have described, coupled with a set of similar events spread over a period of forty days, coupled with the inferences which we may draw from the behaviour of the dead prophet's followers, immediately afterwards, coupled with a living tradition which has been handed down, from that century to this, by a body of men singularly tenacious of tradition, establishes the supernatural character of the mission with which Jesus of Nazareth went about nineteen hundred years ago (*PS,* 390).

The Resurrection offers not only proof but hope. In developing this theme, Knox has as his apologetic target not so much the head as the heart. The risen Christ offers a twofold hope, for our destiny and for our daily lives. He gives us the assurance of victory over death and the prospect of a new creation in this life.

The risen Christ did not simply convince his followers that he had risen; he convinced them that *they* would rise, and they spread throughout the world living a life of heroic self-sacrifice in order to bear witness to this conviction (*PS,* 400). Just as the eternal generation of the divine Word is the first echo breaking the silence of heaven, so "the Resurrection of Jesus Christ is the first echo which breaks the silence after the long sleep of death which has gone on undisturbed since Adam fell" (*PS,* 502).

This echo reaches back to all the just who have come before Jesus. In a sermon on Holy Saturday, Knox paints the picture of King David waiting and watching through the long centuries of twilight for his deliverance. Suddenly the door swings open, and in a blaze of light, he sees "the figure so often, in his poetic imaginings, ah, how dimly foreshadowed, the martyred Christ, wounds shining on hands and feet!" (*PS,* 383).

This same echo reverberates today. In one Easter sermon, Knox invites his listeners to call to mind their deceased friends and relatives:

> Consider, when you see our Lord represented as rising from the tomb with a banner in his hand, it is the symbol of a military penetration; he, the Victor, in rolling back the stone has made a breach in the enemy's lines, for what? So that the army of his redeemed may pour through at his heels. Or, if you will use St Paul's metaphor, his is the first birth out of death; he has opened the barren womb of extinction, not for himself only, but so as to be the firstborn of many brethren. *Vidi aquam*[11]—our Lord's Resurrection is the opening of the springs, the full river has yet to flow. It broadens out, reaches its fulfillment, in ours (*PS,* 384–85).

The Resurrection not only offers hope for life eternal; it also promises life today. It means that there is something stronger than sin, which offers the gift of a new beginning: "There is no autumn in your soul; as long as you believe in Jesus Christ and in what his Resurrection has done for you, it is always spring" (*CSM,* 123). Life for the Christian of any age or condition is always new; the perpetual renovation of our nature is always possible (*PS,* 395). The Church celebrates this newness in her liturgy. At the Easter Vigil,

> a new spark must be struck from the flint, to light a new set of candles and lamps; new holy water must be blessed, and a new font; fresh cloths are spread on the altars, and the

---

[11] "I saw water flowing from the right side of the Temple"—the verse sung while the people are sprinkled with holy water at the beginning of Mass during the Easter Season.

tabernacle itself, on Easter morning, is full of freshly consecrated Hosts. We are beginning all over again, making all
things new. And we have a right to do so, for in the order
of grace there is perpetual novelty. In the order of nature
there is perpetual affectation of novelty, which never comes
to anything; there is nothing new, the wise man reminds us,
under the sun, however much, at the moment, things look
different. Whereas in the order of grace there is no change
apparent, but in truth it is a perpetual spring, inexhaustible
in its fecundity (*PS*, 392).

To perceive "perpetual spring" where there is no apparent change holds out hope, but it also presents a challenge.
The Gospel accounts offer evidence, the desires of the heart
testify to a need, but it requires an act of the will to recognize the risen Jesus today. The tensions and anxieties we
experience make us like the disciples that first Easter night,
hiding behind locked doors. It is a challenge to hear the
risen Christ speaking "Peace!" to our troubled hearts:

He, who three nights ago rebuked them for sleeping while
he agonized, seems now to rebuke them for agonizing while
he sleeps. They should be enjoying the peace of his sabbath,
instead of giving way to the agitation of those unquiet alarms
(*OS*, 16).

For us, as for the first disciples, the sacraments represent
a privileged rendezvous with the risen Christ. When we
receive Holy Communion, we are like the disciples on the
Emmaus road, offering hospitality to the risen Lord, hidden from our sight (*PS*, 268). Contemplating the Blessed
Sacrament in the monstrance, Knox sees in it a veiled manifestation of the risen and glorified body of Jesus, a window
between the world of time and the world of eternity (*PS*,
204). Important as these sacramental encounters are, Knox

tells his listeners that they must also seek the risen Lord in daily life, since this is how he first appeared to his followers:

> You went to the garden to mourn a friend lost, and you found him whom your soul loved. You hid in the upper room, and locked the doors on yourselves; you looked round and he was there. You met a Stranger by the roadside, got into conversation with him, entertained him, and there was just a turning of the head, a familiar gesture, and you knew him. You went fishing on the lake; somebody hailed you, and told you how to cast your nets better; and even as you struggled with your sudden catch, it occurred to you, "Where have I heard that authoritative ring in the voice before?" And all in the moment the truth flashed on you. Doesn't that mean, possibly, that heaven is a good deal nearer to us than we know? (*US,* 340).

THE INCARNATION

If the Christian tradition is genuine, a misleading entry—not a false entry, according to the custom of the times, but a misleading entry—was made in the registrar's returns for Palestine one winter's day, getting on for two thousand years ago. The baby registered at Bethlehem as the son of one Joseph, carpenter, of Nazareth, was in fact nothing of the kind. What had really happened? The second Person of the Blessed Trinity had assumed, taken to himself, a human nature; a body, miraculously borne in the womb of a Virgin, with nerve-centres, brain, memory, will, intellect, and all the rest of our human make-up complete. But not a human personality; not that innermost fortress of identity which the legal-minded Latins thought of as constituting a person, the subject of human acts, while the metaphysical Greeks thought of it as a mere ultimate principle of reality. There were not two people here, a man and a God who after some fashion dwelt in him; there was a single Person who existed simultaneously in two different contexts; he reigned in heaven, and lay there on the straw.

The mysteries of the Christian religion come to us in majestic isolation as known facts, guaranteed to us by an authority which does not abide our question. But they have, for all that, a pre-history and a history. A pre-history, because God did not leave himself without witness in the unredeemed world; men were left to search for him, and somehow to grope their way towards him. Not *all* their guesses about theology could be a hundred per cent wrong; there would be some foreshadowing of the truth. And a history,

Ronald Knox, "The Incarnation", unpublished conference, typescript, n.d., Knox Papers, Mells, Somerset.

because they came to us in the rough, these mysteries, and
they must be polished by the hammer of controversy before
their delicate facets took the light. So it is with this mystery
of the Incarnation. It didn't come into the pagan world quite
unheralded; men had dreamed of something like it, though
they had not dared to dream that it might be true. And on
the other hand, it did not take its present verbal form until
a theological war had been waged over it, and councils had
met to discuss the use of a preposition. We shall understand
the precise implications of it better, I think, if we give some
attention to all this. We shall appreciate the craftsmanship of
its definition, if we have put it side by side with the export
rejects; with the notions that were superseded as inadequate,
and the notions that were rejected as erroneous.

Man has made god in his own likeness—the cheap sneer
is as old as Lucretius. But the pagans, however much they
might think of their gods as like men, were nevertheless
conscious of a huge gulf between the human and the divine. Even the Greeks, so shamelessly anthropomorphic,
felt that; the gods were the immortals, set over against mor-
tal men; hope was the only goddess left in the world, the
rest had all gone off to Olympus, leaving us in the lurch.
Was there, then, any possibility of bridging that gulf? They
liked to think so, and their legends bear pathetic witness
to their preoccupation with the idea. How full mythology
is of divine theophanies, of gods who appeared in human
form amongst men! When St Paul performed a miracle at
Lystra, he and St Barnabas were greeted with cries of "It
is the gods, who have come down to us in the likeness of
men!" The good people of Lystra don't seem particularly
surprised; they know all about the protocol to be observed
on such occasions—sacrifice will have to be offered by the
priest of Jupiter, Defender of the City; that is the form. Had
not the same two gods appeared to Baucis and Philemon in

the legend? Yes, it is thought of as quite possible that the gods might want to consort with men; only—what is the use of it? They will go back the way they came, and gods will be gods and men will be men still. A kind of flying arch has been thrown out, but the gulf has not been bridged.

On that side, the theophanies; on the other side, apotheosis. There was abundant precedent in classical mythology for the idea that a man who had deserved well in his lifetime, Romulus, for example, might be raised to a sort of divine status after death. *Hac arte Pollux et vagus Hercules*[1]— the thing was notorious. And, as we know, about the same time when true religion dawned upon the world, it became the thing to pretend that one Roman Emperor after another underwent this process of apotheosis, and became a suitable object for worship. "I rather think I am becoming a god", said Vespasian, the honest man, on his death-bed; but no satire, even that of Seneca, would put a stop to it. How much did those pagans really believe in their stuff? Again and again the question poses itself, always declining to be answered. Anyhow, in the life-time of the Apostles it was the common affectation of the world to pretend that Olympus was being gradually populated with faded voluptuaries who had worn the purple. Even so, what was the use of it? The gulf was being bridged from the other end, from man's end; but the slave who prostrated himself before the altar of *divus Tiberius* was no more personally interested than the tramp who reads, in some newspaper, the autobiography of a millionaire. Theophanies which happened once in a blue moon, apotheosis which fell to the lot of a national figure now and again; were not "man" and "god" still utterly disparate terms in spite of it?

[1] Horace, *Odes* 3:3. The poet praises strength of will, by which means Pollux and Hercules attained the heavenly glories in which one day Augustus will drink nectar.

Now, imagine such a pagan, with all the disillusionment of a decadent pagan world filling his thoughts, to have come across, and read, the four gospels. In many ways, from one angle or another, their language would seem familiar. "All those who did welcome him, he empowered to become the children of God"—this was the language of theophany; did not Philemon and Baucis have something of the same experience, when they were rewarded for their hospitality to Zeus and Hermes? And then he would turn back from the first chapter of St John to the 12th chapter of St Luke, where he would read, "it is fire I have come to spread over the earth, and what better wish can I have than that it should be kindled?" Was not this an echo of the legend about Prometheus, who climbed up to heaven to bring down, for mankind's use, the gift of fire? Only, how exactly *were* we to think of him, this Christ who had moved so enigmatically through the world, only yesterday? Was he a divine visitant who had come and gone? Or was he a man who had overpassed, somehow, the limits of mortality? On which side of the gulf had his flying arch been thrown out? And at last our pagan would begin to realize that, in the unconscious assumption of the men who wrote the gospels, their Hero was one who had combined the two roles, who had linked God with man and man with God simultaneously. He was God already, when he hung upon the Cross. He was Man still, when he ascended into heaven. The flying arches had been thrown out from both sides, and had met in the middle. *Habemus Pontificem.*[2]

And all this without commentary, without a hint of theologizing. The writers of the gospels were not at pains to

[2] Literally, "We have a bridge-maker." In ancient Rome, "pontiff" was a name given to priests, who were held to be a bridge between the earthly and heavenly realms. The Vulgate uses the term *Pontifex* for the Jewish high priest and applies it to Christ in the Letter to the Hebrews.

say at one point, "See, how fully human he was!" or at another point, "How could this be accounted for, unless he were divine?" They simply told their story, without betraying any consciousness of embarrassment, without attempting to meet the challenge of incredulity. True, St John had prefixed to *his* gospel a prologue which speaks of Christ as existing from the first in the bosom of his Father, and you expected to meet, here at any rate, nothing but the language of theophany. Yet it was this same gospel which went out of its way to stress the other side of the paradox; nowhere else did you read how Christ had sat down to rest from human weariness; how he wept for human sorrow at the news of a friend's death; nowhere else was he reported as so constantly professing obedience to a Father greater than himself. Unless you are prepared to rewrite the gospels, or to mutilate them beyond recognition, this composite picture has to be accepted. And even when you turn to St Paul, and the other documents of the New Testament, the same anomaly meets you everywhere. The epistle to the Hebrews, like the fourth Gospel, begins with a flourish of theophany; Christ is described here as "a Son who is the radiance of his Father's splendour, and the full expression of his being; all creation depends, for its support, on his enabling word". Yet, a few chapters later, we read in the same epistle, "Christ during his earthly life, offered prayer and entreaty to the God who could save him from death, not without a piercing cry, not without tears; yet with much piety as won him a hearing. Son of God though he was, he learned obedience in the school of suffering"—is not this, par excellence, a *human* Christ?

Do not say that the Evangelists took their cue from the other New Testament writers, or the other New Testament writers from the Evangelists. Both alike took their cue from the tradition of the Christian Church, already beginning to harden, but still attested by living memories. The reason, I think, why the staggering doctrine of God-made-Man is assumed by the New Testament writers with so little ado, is that they took it over from witnesses who had been personally acquainted with God-made-Man, and to those witnesses the justice of the claim was apparent. There was no need to argue; the human Christ they knew, and the Divine Christ in whom they had learned to believe, were somehow part of a single experience. At the very end of his life, the very last of the Apostles felt it was time to set that on record: "No spirit" writes St John in his first epistle, "no spirit which would disunite Jesus comes from God". That is the only reading which is critically tolerable; to *disunite* Jesus, to introduce a kind of astigmatism into the Church's memories of the God-Man, so that the bridge is not a bridge after all —*that*, he tells us, is the spirit of Antichrist.

The definition of this mystery which is familiar to us, that which asserts one Person and two natures in the Incarnate, was hammered out for us by centuries of controversy. And to this day there are Nestorian Christians in Asia who will not accept the one Person; Monophysite Christians, chiefly in Egypt, who will not accept the two natures. Curiously, it remains uncertain whether the quarrel, when it started, was one of doctrines or merely one of words. For whereas the Latins of the west used terms whose meaning was obvious, the Greeks could never be certain that they were using terms in the same sense. But, whatever beliefs either party really held, it remains true that some such definition had to be made. Both before and after the days of the great Christological controversy, men have been tempted to rationalize away the mystery of the Incarnation, by denying one half or the other of the paradox. Rationalize away, and in a sense paganize away; because in the last resort they are falling back on the old pagan guesses, and degrading the Incarnation to the status of a mere theophany, or a mere apotheosis.

I think I've been told that if you shut one eye, you see everything just as clearly as you could see it with two eyes, only you see it in two dimensions instead of three. For heaven's sake don't come and tell me whether this is true or not. Whether it is true or not, it is surely true that we ought to contemplate the mystery of the Incarnation not with the eye of faith, but with the two eyes of faith. I mean that when we read the gospels we ought to read them as the biography of God-made-Man, not thinking of our Lord as God or as Man in isolation. It's so easy for some of us—it all depends on the way you're made, like being a little Calvinist or else a little Pelagian—it's so easy for some of us to forget about our Lord's Humanity when we read the gospels. I mean, you start by saying to yourself, "He was God; of course, in some mysterious way he had concentrated his divine presence within the limits of a human body; he looked, seemed, just like anybody else. But really, of course, that was just his condescension. When we are told that he grew in knowledge, that means that he behaved as if he were growing in knowledge; he only made a gradual disclosure of the knowledge which, since he was God, he possessed from the very first. When we are told that he was moved with indignation, that he wondered, that he wept, we mean that he expressed indignation, that he described himself as wondering, that he allowed himself to weep. In the garden of Gethsemani, he went through the motions of a spiritual conflict, as if there were a human will that had to be brought into line with the will of God, whereas in fact there was only a divine will, reacting as a divine will inevitably would. When he 'died' on the Cross, what he actually did was to withdraw his divine presence from the perishable human body he had assumed, which thereupon became lifeless." You see, it is all a two-dimensional picture; there has been no Incarnation, only a theophany.

Alternatively, you may start at the human end. It is perhaps permissible, but only by way of paradox, to describe the Virgin Mary as the Mother of God. The Son who was born to her was not so much God as the perfect vehicle of Deity. He was a human Person, who grew up like the rest of us, although *his* was, from the first dawn of reason, a life of perfect dedication. At some moment of his career, probably when he was baptized in the river Jordan, the divine influence descended upon him, not partially and transiently, but in a fullness of which we have no comprehension. So fully did it possess him, so completely did he identify himself with it, that he would describe himself, more than once, as having come down from the Father, and going back to the Father; it came natural to him to talk like that, but in reality he was not speaking of himself personally, only of the divine presence which dwelt in him. Personally, he remained man, and capable of sin—that is the whole point of the Agony in Gethsemani. When he had endured the final test of death, and had been raised to life again, the Divine indwelling became more manifest than ever, so that his followers did not scruple to refer to him as God. And indeed, it is in that human shrine, in which he tabernacled among us, that we worship to this day the second Person of the Blessed Trinity. Language like that, if they would be honest with themselves, would express the thought of many people to-day who regard themselves as Christians. But it is the language of apotheosis, not of Incarnation.

The bridge has got to be safe-guarded at both ends; and the sentinel on their bridge-head is the doctrine of the hypostatic union—one Person, two natures. We are sometimes apt to feel a scruple, or if we don't feel it ourselves, our neighbours suggest it to us, about the use of philosophical terms in defining the faith. Ever since philosophy gave up talking the language of the Middle Ages, this objection has been made; and it is made all the more violently in modern Oxford, where it has become the fashion not merely to ask people what they mean by their use of terms, but whether they mean anything. "Nature" for example, is by derivation what we are born with; how can God have a Nature, since God was not born? "Person" means literally an actor's mask, and therefore a character or role in a play; why do we use the term as if it means something individual, incommunicable? Well, obviously we haven't time to discuss ultimate difficulties like that this morning. But I think *for our present purposes* it is fair to say that the old terms are good enough to symbolize the truth of the doctrine we are asserting, just as the Swiss Guards, who don't wear battle-dress or carry tommy-guns, are good enough to symbolize the dignity of the Holy Father. You see, we didn't pretend that when theologians started talking about person and nature it gave us any deeper insight into the positive meaning of the Incarnation. They didn't help us to understand what the doctrine of the Incarnation *was*; they only helped us to understand what it was *not*; they were notices put up to warn the heretics, in language which the heretics themselves could construe. If modern philosophy will devise for us an alternative language, more accurate than the old, we shall be delighted to use it. But the old terms, with the history they have behind them, are a sufficient index of the Church's mind. God made Man, not God made like Man; God made Man, not Man made God—that is the point.

13

"THE BREATHLESS CONFIDENCES
OF LIVING MEN": THE RELIABILITY
OF THE NEW TESTAMENT

The person and mission of Jesus are at the heart of Christian apologetics. But how can he be encountered, when two thousand years and thousands of miles separate us from the events of first-century Palestine? Jesus is met in the community of followers that has borne witness to him since his lifetime; this community has been authorized by Christ to preach in his name. This authority, so important for Knox, will be discussed in the next chapter. But in his apologetic schema, that question is preceded by a consideration of the credibility of the New Testament records concerning Christ, which is the subject of this chapter.

Knox exhorts his ideal apologist to

> read the New Testament, not as a set of "passages" which must somehow be reconciled with one another, but as the breathless confidences of living men, reacting to human situations, and inflamed with zeal for their Master (*PGNA*, 16).

Inasmuch as the authors of the New Testament are "inflamed with zeal for their Master," it is impossible to distinguish between the New Testament as an ordinary human document and the New Testament as an inspired document of faith. At the same time, this dichotomy is necessary to some extent in apologetics. The meaning of the life of Christ is found in the faith and teaching of the Church; the facts of that life and their effect on the first disciples are chronicled in documents that can be studied *as* documents.

How reliable are these documents? Knox formulates his response along two lines, arguing that the writings of the New Testament are trustworthy from both a literary and a human point of view.

Literary Evidence

As a student of the classics and a master of English prose, Knox was well qualified to present a literary defense of the New Testament. His work in translating the Bible made him even more sensitive to its stylistic variations. In his conferences and in his *New Testament Commentary*, he underscored the very human origins of the biblical literature.

Knox compares the New Testament to a brilliantly colored illustration in a child's picture book. Just as the picture is created by three different printings of red, yellow, and blue, so the New Testament consists of three levels: oral tradition, Gospels, other writings (*PS,* 486).

The Oral Tradition

Concerning this stratum, Knox has little to say. It is reflected in the common tradition behind the Synoptic Gospels and contains material about the broad outlines of Jesus' life and teaching. The Gospels were written on the basis of this tradition "before the scent has had time to grow cold", and in replacing the oral tradition, killed it (*BC,* 80).

The Gospels

As a translator and commentator, Knox recognized that the Gospels present difficulties to the modern student: apparent contradictions; sayings of Jesus that can be challenged on historical grounds; sayings that are obscure or cryptic; stories that are similar but not identical; variant readings in manuscripts.[1] Knox had a somewhat idiosyncratic approach to exegesis and did not consider himself a biblical scholar. His *New Testament Commentary* is best appreciated as a work not of exegesis but of apologetics; his object is to examine such difficulties as may present themselves to the ordinary person.

Concerning the thorny question of the interdependence of the Synoptic Gospels, he observes that whatever the exact explanation may be, it is clear that there was a standard tradition the Evangelists used as a skeleton for their narratives, fleshing it out with independent traditions available to each. The general picture of Jesus in these independent sources is not unlike that which is found in the common tradition. Whatever problems may arise in comparing the Gospels, the broad outline of the life and teaching of Jesus is the same (*US,* 209–10).

For Ronald Knox, the Gospels are literature that *rings true*. He concludes one of his Oxford conferences by saying:

> The documents of the New Testament are documents that belong to real life, not to an elaborate literary fraud. Read any of the apocryphal gospels, and I think you will see what I mean (*US,* 210–11).

---

[1] Ronald Knox, *New Testament Commentary*, vol. 1: *The Gospels* (London: Burns and Oates, 1953), p. vii.

Other New Testament Writings

Although he wrote commentaries on the Catholic Epistles
and the Apocalypse, Knox has far more to say about Saint
Paul. Leaving out the four Gospels, most of the New Testament comes from the mind of this one man (*PS,* 485).
As to the authorship of the letters attributed to Paul, Knox
maintains in *The Belief of Catholics* that they all come from
his hand (*BC,* 77); in his later Oxford conferences, he is
more cautious on this point (*US,* 207). But the earlier epistles are authentic, not simply in the sense that Paul wrote
them but also in the sense that they were real letters—"you
feel the actualities of the situation tingling in every line he
writes" (*US,* 207).

Knox likens reading these letters to overhearing a telephone conversation:

> A great deal of it is all meaningless to you, but every now
> and then some piece of information emerges which you had
> no idea of; you gather that your hostess' husband has been
> knighted, or that she is just bringing out a book on fossils,
> or that it's her birthday today—something of that sort. Well,
> the theology of St Paul leaks out rather like that (*US,* 206–7).

And what is the nature of this "overheard" theology?

> Good old undenominational Christianity, with all the hard
> parts left out, agreed-upon syllabus sort of stuff? Not a bit, it's
> all there, pitilessly brandished over the heads of the unfortu-
> nate Philippians, most of whom probably didn't know how to
> spell. The doctrine of the Holy Trinity keeps on coming in;
> it's a kind of refrain that runs in St Paul's head. The doctrine
> of the Incarnation of God made Man, is everywhere treated as
> the only possible explanation of the world around us, of the
> whole course of history. St Paul doesn't introduce them to
> the doctrine of the Holy Eucharist, say, or the Resurrection

of the Body, as if he were instructing them; he treats these things as a matter of course—they only need to be reminded about them. The whole Christian thing is there already.[2]

But Paul is not only valuable as a witness to first-century Christian theology. His letters also dovetail with the Gospels in presenting a picture of Christ. This idea seems strange at first, because the whole of Jesus' earthly biography passes unnoticed by Paul, other than his birth under the Law and his death. He quotes no sermon of Jesus in his letters, draws no illustrations from his ministry. Yet he brings the Gospel portrait of Jesus to life:

> Why did the Apostles leave their nets and follow without a word, when our Lord said "Follow me"? What was the magic of voice or look that drew them away, in those early days when no miracles had yet been done, when the campaign of preaching had not yet been opened? Something escapes us in the narrative; what we call, in the loose sense, "personality." . . . The tremendous impact which his force of character made on people—do you remember how, according to St John, his captors in the garden went back and fell on the ground when he said, "I am Jesus of Nazareth"? —all that is difficult to realize in the Synoptists. It becomes easier to realize when you watch the effect it had on St Paul; how, after the interview on the Damascus road, he saw Christ in everyone, Christ in everything, nothing but Christ (*US*, 216).

Human Evidence

The letters of Paul are an authentic reflection of his encounter with the risen Christ. It is this kind of experience

[2] Ronald Knox, "The New Testament Record", unpublished conference, typescript, 1952, Mells, Somerset, pp. 2–3; see pp. 202–11 of this book.

that lies behind the entire New Testament record. Knox emphasizes the reliability of these writings by drawing our attention to the events that lay behind them.

In one sense, the Easter encounters were unique; the appearances of the risen Christ were limited to a certain time and place. In another sense, they are accessible to us because they were human encounters and thus analogous in some way to our common experience. For example, when reflecting on Paul's meeting with Christ on the Damascus road, Knox asks his congregation:

> Do you know what it is to meet some great man, or even some interesting personality that arrests you, and to go away quite forgetting how he was dressed or even what he looked like, because the inspiration of what he was saying riveted you at the time, so that you were unconscious of anything else? And afterwards, even what he said hardly remains in the memory; what exactly *did* he say? (*PS,* 489).

In the same way, he tells the schoolgirls at Aldenham that they should not be surprised at discrepancies found in the accounts of the first Easter. It is common, when we have gone through an exciting experience, to remember many odd details and forget important things. When they think back on their wedding day, they will probably remember how the best man's collar came loose from his shirt at the back, and be very vague about whether they said, "I will" or "I won't" (*CSM,* 127).

This human element is central not only to the events of the New Testament but to the composition of the written records. In describing the formation of the oral tradition behind the Gospels, Knox writes:

> We are not to think of the twelve Apostles as a set of pressmen at a conference, each of them eager to get to the telephone

first and put his story through. Think, rather of some meal you have taken with a religious community, and how they sat around afterwards and told stories of old Father So-and-so, now dead; how some of the stories, to the community, were chestnuts, and there were others which the young ones hadn't heard before. That is the sort of atmosphere in which the stories of the Founder are cradled. . . . The Gospel as preached by the Apostles was a very brief outline; you get it in the Acts, you get it in First Corinthians. But, as they met day after day, of course the Apostles talked over old times and exchanged memories of what our Lord said and did— especially of what he said, because we are all apt to forget conversations (*US*, 209).

Ronald Knox did not doubt for a moment that the New Testament is inspired by the Holy Spirit. But the biblical accounts are also very "human" evidence, both in terms of how they mediate the experience of the first Christians and in the way the books themselves came to be written. They are truly "the breathless confidences of living men, reacting to human situations, and inflamed with zeal for their Master".

THE NEW TESTAMENT RECORD

What we've got to talk about this morning is the genuineness of the New Testament record. The word *record* has got an ugly sound for most of us; at the back of our minds—in these days of gramophones and of wireless—we contrast it with the living voice. And if we are not careful we shall fall into the error which nearly all non-Catholics fall into; the error, I mean, of forgetting that the Church has a living voice. It isn't true that the Bible and the Fathers are the only evidence we have for believing in the Christian religion. Even if nothing at all had ever been entrusted to paper, there would have been a living Christian tradition handed down from mother to son across the centuries, learned by students in seminaries and preached by priests from the pulpit. Of course, it is quite true that an oral tradition like that very easily gets furred over with legend and speculation, so that we have to be grateful to Providence for the writings of the Fathers, and still more for the inspired documents of Scripture. But for all that, the precise thing which you and I, as Catholics, accept as the faith of Christ is not a document or a set of documents, in the first instance, but a living tradition from which all our Christian documents sprang. Christianity isn't the religion of a book, as Mohammedanism is the religion of a book; our Lord didn't leave a line in writing and (as far as we know) he never told his Apostles to. He left a tradition which has gone on ever since; only, at frequent intervals, this tradition has been pin-pointed for us by being set down on paper. And that applies even to the New Testament records. We have to think of them not in isolation, as

Ronald Knox, "The New Testament Record", unpublished conference, typescript, 1952, Knox Papers, Mells, Somerset.

if they had been washed up in a bottle from some unknown desert island, but as the thoughts of Christian people like ourselves, only uttered hundreds and hundreds of years ago.

That's especially true of St Paul's epistles, which demonstrably belong to a period when the Crucifixion and the Ascension lay within living memory. The extraordinary thing about St Paul's epistles is that here you have a man caught off his guard. He wasn't thinking, as he wrote, about you and me. He was having a row with his converts about their insubordination, or whipping them up to contribute more generously to the collections, and quite incidentally, quite off the record, he introduced staggering pieces of theology. There's that great passage in Philippians which has kept theologians busy ever since discussing the light it throws on the mystery of the Incarnation; why did he write that? Why, because two old ladies at Philippi were quarreling and he wanted to give them a lesson in humility. Reading those epistles isn't like listening to a broadcast; it's like overhearing a conversation on the telephone. Of course, there are disadvantages about that; we all know how maddening it can be sitting in the room while somebody at the telephone says "No!. . . No!. . . Did he really?. . . Who?. . . I said 'Who?' . . . Oh, him!" and so on. It has its disadvantages, of course, listening to St Paul like that, because very often we can only get the sketchiest idea of what he's talking about. But on the other side, you see what an advantage it is to take him off his guard. He is striding up and down the room in a great hurry, dictating almost without thinking what he is saying, as likely as not leaving out the main verb in the sentence; there is nothing carefully prepared, he isn't taking down the Summa all the time to see what St Thomas thought about it; he deals merely with the commonplaces of theology as they were understood by him—and presumably as they would be understood by the Christians he was writing to—just round about 50 A.D.

What is it, this primitive theology which escapes from him in casual asides like that? Good old undenominational Christianity, with all the hard parts left out, agreed-upon syllabus sort of stuff? Not a bit, it's all there, pitilessly brandished over the heads of the unfortunate Philippians, most of whom probably didn't know how to spell. The doctrine of the Holy Trinity keeps on coming in; it's a kind of refrain that runs in St Paul's head. The doctrine of the Incarnation of God made Man, is everywhere treated as the only possible explanation of the world around us, of the whole course of history. St Paul doesn't introduce them to the doctrine of the Holy Eucharist, say, or the Resurrection of the Body, as if he were instructing them; he treats these things as a matter of course—they only need to be reminded about them. The whole Christian thing is there already.

And what he leaves out is almost more extraordinary than what the puts in. You would have expected to hear a great deal about the way our Lord lived on earth, how he went about doing good, how he rebuked the pride of the Pharisees, how he prayed for his murderers, how he prophesied the destruction of Jerusalem. But there is nothing about all that, hardly anything about his life except the fact that he died and rose again. The life of Christ is not a story to be told, it is a power working in the Christian. How often do you think St Paul quotes our Lord? He gives us the words of Institution, not another word of his from end to end of the epistles. And yet he was writing with St Luke at his side, St Luke, writing his gospel probably at that very moment. By St Paul, the whole biography of the Incarnate is taken for granted; it seems to have been swamped, crowded out, by the theology of the Incarnation.

And then, when you turn to the first three gospels, you find that by one of those strange coincidences which are almost too strange to be coincidences, it is all just the other way about. You are told the story of a child born in a country town, of a man who went out into the wilderness to be tried out by the devil, and you are left to piece out your theology of the Incarnation as best you can from biographical data of that kind; the Evangelists aren't going to dot the I's and cross the T's for you. Here's a single instance which shews you the kind of thing I mean. In the time when St Paul wrote—you can tell it in every page of his writings—the usual way of referring to the Incarnate Son of God was "the Lord". And you can catch St Luke falling into that very natural habit, all through his Gospel. Not when he is going over the same ground as the earlier Evangelists, and following their model. But if he has a story of his own to tell, you find him saying "when the Lord saw her, he had compassion on her", or something like that; it comes at least a dozen times. But the two earlier Evangelists, St Matthew and St Mark, never talk about "the Lord"; they always call him Jesus. Not that they wrote earlier than St Paul, not that they weren't accustomed to the title. But when St Matthew, or St Mark who had St Peter to guide him, sat down to write about the old days, they unconsciously saw their Hero as men saw him, as a Man amongst men; described him, therefore, not by the title his friends used (even then), but by the name he bore in public. That's a phenomenon which, I think, hasn't been given nearly as much attention as it deserves. Because the name or the title you use in describing a person slips out while you aren't thinking. If you put force on yourself to use, artificially, the name that doesn't come natural to you, the name that does come natural to you slips out unawares—as it did with St Luke.

I don't think we shall do a good service to truth if we try to make out that the first three gospels are primitive in the sense of being wholly unsophisticated, wholly art-less, wholly (what they call nowadays) objective. It used to be maintained that St Mark was, whereas St Matthew and St Luke weren't; but more recently people have begun to trace patterns even in St Mark; he too, it seems, narrated the events of our Lord's life not as bare events, but as part of a Providential arrangement. Well, of course that lies on the surface. All the Evangelists were concerned to point out that our Lord's life fulfilled, whether in its general outlines or in matters of detail, the Old Testament prophecies about the Messiah. St John will even be at pains to describe how the legs of the two crucified thieves were broken, merely to emphasize the fact that our Lord's bones were not broken —like the bones of the paschal lamb. And again, they will give prominence to sayings of his, parables of his, which foreshadowed the rejection of the Jews and the call of the Gentiles. They wrote, it seems, with a purpose, not merely as chroniclers.

But all that, you see, while it may suggest that the first three gospels were not primitive in the sense of being artless or "objective", does strongly suggest that they were prim-itive in the sense of belonging to a very early stage in the development of Church history. Because the argument from Old Testament prophecy, although it might commend itself to a Gentile as perfectly valid, would appeal much more to a *Jewish* reader as belonging to a familiar world of thought; this was where he came in. And if you suspect the first three gospels of trying to justify the ways of God to men in rejecting his ancient people and replacing it by a universal Church, that surely belongs to the very earliest stratum of Christian propaganda. I don't say that the acute conflict between the Jewish and the Gentile element within the Christian body came to an end all of a sudden when Jerusalem was destroyed in A.D. 70, but I think it's obvious that by that time the force of it was spent. Again and again, if you will look beneath the surface of the gospels, you will find the same problems being tackled which St Paul tackled in his epistles to the churches of Galatia and of Rome.

And indeed, I don't see how anybody could read the gospel of St Matthew without *parti pris*, without some theological or critical axe to grind, and give it a date after 70 A.D. Twice in the course of it, once when he is describing the temptation and once when he is describing the crucifixion, he refers to Jerusalem as "the holy city"; nowhere else is it called that in the New Testament. That is perfectly natural on the lips of a Jewish Christian who writes while Jerusalem is still standing; for the author of the Apocalypse, the holy city was the new Jerusalem, eternal in the heavens; Matthew, born and bred in Judaea, takes a kind of unconscious pride in the old Jerusalem; it murders the prophets, it has murdered Jesus Christ, but to him it is the holy city still. That is either the most natural thing in the world, or else one of the most elaborate fakes in the whole of literature. Again, in referring to the piece of land which the chief priests bought with Judas' thirty pieces of silver, he tells us that it is called "the field of blood" to this day. To this day—was anybody going to remember these bits of local lore about Jerusalem when the city itself lay a heap of ruins? And again, in St Matthew— only in St Matthew—you are suddenly presented with the statement that the people who collect the florin came up and asked St Peter whether his Master paid the florin. What florin? No footnote, you see, nothing in the way of an explanation. We know, of course, that the florin was a contribution made for the upkeep of the Temple. But when the

Temple had fallen down, and there was no more question
of upkeeping it, is it possible that any author should have
written about "the florin" just like that, as if his readers were
certain to know what he meant?

That's St Matthew, and I think you can make out the same
sort of case for St Mark—though of course he was writing
for Gentiles; in Rome, tradition says; and you wouldn't expect him to betray his Jewish origin as St Matthew does.
But it's St Mark who tells us, when he mentions Simon of
Cyrene helping to carry the Cross, "By the way, he was
the father of Alexander and Rufus". Who on earth, we ask,
were Alexander and Rufus? Nothing known, except that in
the last chapter of Romans St Paul sends his love to Rufus. . . . Oh, it was a fairly common name; but why did St
Mark mention this relationship, if not because it would interest his Roman readers? And why should it interest them,
if Rufus was already dead and gone? With St Luke, as we've
seen, the case is rather different; and if we had no other
evidence we shouldn't be certain that he wrote before the
fall of Jerusalem. But it's clear that he wrote it before the
Acts; and it isn't easy to see why St Luke should finish up
the Acts where he does, unless you suppose that he finished
it off at the moment of writing. And that was well before
70 A.D.

By ordinary probabilities, then, the first three Evangelists
were writing about things within living memory; just as I
should be if I wrote about the 1914 War. But were they
telling the truth? Or rather—for a confusion or a misap-
prehension here and there wouldn't matter for our present
purposes—were they *out* to tell the truth? Or were they just
making a good story of it?

Well, of course you can try them out by merely mechanical tests; do they agree with one another? Do their allusions

to contemporary events, to geography, to Jewish customs and so on bear the stamp of truth? But when you've fought your way through a forest of details like that, you aren't much nearer. A man can mug up his setting all right, and yet be distorting his facts. In the last resort, the only way to make a guess whether your author is telling the truth or not is to read him right through, and then shut your eyes and ask yourself, "Is that the real thing?" And if you do that with the first three gospels, you get a most curious result. You find that they have been doing the exact opposite of what they would have done if they had been out to tell lies about it all. They have given you the biography of a *man*.

You see, it's all very well, but it is quite certain that St Paul preached Jesus Christ as the eternal Son of God. For him, as we were saying, the theology of the Incarnation seems to blot out the biography of the Incarnate; he doesn't tell us about it; we no longer know Christ, he tells us, "after the flesh", that is to say, in a human context; he is too intimately bound up with our prayer-life for that. Now, here were these contemporaries of St Paul sitting down to write the biography of our Lord, of God Incarnate. If they had simply had a rough outline to guide them, and had been building up the story to their own specifications, they might perhaps have turned out something like the Gospel of St John, but they couldn't have turned out anything like the first three gospels. They would have been straining every nerve to make their Hero look Divine. And what they have done is to make him look human.

St Paul tells me that God became Man; the Evangelists tell me that he became *a* Man. Not merely in the sense that he belongs to his background; that the sort of proverbs he quoted, the sort of references he made to the Scriptures, the sort of illustrations he used in his teaching, were all in character; not beyond the compass, ideally anyhow, of a Galilean peasant. They tell me more than that; how God made Man was God made a Boy, who grew in wisdom with the years; how he underwent baptism, the baptism which was ordained for the remission of sins; how he was tempted by the devil; how he was surprised, and asked questions; how he chose a scoundrel to be one of his most intimate friends; how he wept with disappointment over the infidelity of Jerusalem; how he shrank from the near approach of death; how he complained aloud, on his Cross, that God had forsaken him. And as paradox after paradox comes out, the theologians sit there making it all right, and saying, "Here we distinguish; in one sense yes, and in another sense no", but the Evangelists just go on with their story; "we don't know about that" they explain; "all we known is that this is what happened".

Our Lord, in the epistles, perfect God; our Lord, in the gospels, perfect Man. I'm not trying to prove the truth of the hypostatic Union; I'm simply drawing your attention to the curious way the two accounts dovetail in. I'm only arguing that if St Matthew, St Mark and St Luke were writing apocryphal gospels, it is the most extraordinary thing in the history of literature, because the way in which they wrote is exactly the way in which apocrypha is *not* written. I've taken up all my time without making any attempt to deal with the rest of the New Testament; the Acts of the Apostles, for example, for which you could reconstruct the whole of the Christian creed, pretty well, even if the rest of the Bible had perished. And, of course, that tantalizing document, the Gospel of St John. Don't, please, go away with the impression that because I've left St John out of the count, I doubt the truth of his evidence or underestimate the value of it. It's only that the whole question of its authorship and date have become so complicated, through the vast amount of learned books which have been written about it, that you can't work it in a short conference like this. Look out for a book which Faber's are going to publish in the spring, "John who saw", by Adrian Green-Armytage. He was one of the first batch of undergraduates I had here, and now he's a stock-broker, writing popular apologetics. I hope a lot of you will do the same, later on.

14

"THE PATIENT PIONEER": THE TEACHING CHURCH

The New Testament writings record the faith of the early Church, but they are not the legacy of Christ himself. Knox notes that Jesus did not leave behind any writings; what he did leave behind was a community of people authorized to act in his name (*BC*, 120). It is their faith that is captured in the New Testament and their teaching that guarantees the authenticity of these writings. It is through this "living witness" that Christ reaches us, people of a later age. The credibility of this witness is suggested as the fifth and final area of concern for Knox' apologist:

> He will portray the teaching Church, not as a harassed official "handing out" information at a series of press-conferences, but as a patient pioneer washing out gold from the turbid stream of her own memories (*PGNA,* 16–17).

In this first part of this book, we saw how important the teaching authority of the Church was for Ronald Knox. His search for a sure foundation for his faith led him through the painful process of leaving the Church in which he was raised in order to join the Catholic Church. The issue was to be a central one throughout his life, as he sought to share with others the unique claim of the Catholic Church to teach with the authority of Christ.

The Nature of the Church

In order to appreciate Knox' treatment of her teaching office, it will be helpful first to consider his understanding of the nature of the Church. Here we will consider his treatment of the Church in the New Testament, his understanding of her essential characteristics, and of her relation to non-Catholics.

The New Testament

Did Jesus intend to found a Church, that is, a visible society with a particular organization? Knox believes that he did and that there is evidence for this in the New Testament. Actually, he says, it would be more correct to speak of a "refoundation"; the visible community of the Church is built on the remnant of the old Ecclesia of Israel (*BC*, 122–23). The nature of this new Assembly is revealed in the teaching of Jesus, above all in his parables. In these, Jesus identifies this new community with the "Kingdom", not openly but by the use of allegory and allusion.[1] In these parables, Knox discerns three important characteristics of this Kingdom.

First, although it will be a visible society like the old Ecclesia, it will include the Gentiles: the latecomers to the vineyard receive an equal wage, the Elder Son should welcome the Prodigal. In fact, the disbelief of many Jews will be countered by the faith of many Gentiles—the places of the invited guests will be taken by the poor; the vineyard will be taken away from the wicked husbandmen and be given to others (*BC*, 122).

[1] Ronald Knox, "The Organized Church in the New Testament", in *The Religion of the Scriptures*, ed. C. Lattey, S.J. (Cambridge: W. Heffer and Sons, 1921), p. 75.

Secondly, this Kingdom will not appear suddenly. Many of the parables speak of gradual growth, delay in fulfillment:

> And unless the Evangelists have entirely misrepresented his point of view, the "kingdom" is not a sudden event, but a long process followed by a sudden event—herb-growth ending in sickle work, book-keeping followed by audit-day. If our Lord was in a hurry for his "kingdom" to start, it was, surely, the impatience of the farmer to get finished with the sowing and leave the crop to come up; the impatience of the *grand seigneur* to set out on his tour and let his servants prove their mettle (*OR,* 42).

This Kingdom is to act as a leaven gradually influencing the mass of dough, as a mustard seed slowly transforming dead material into a living organism (*PS,* 89). The growth of the Kingdom will require patience; Knox suggests that this is why Jesus called several fishermen to be Apostles (*PS,* 437).

Thirdly, the Kingdom will not be perfect: tares will grow among the wheat; there will be dog-fish in the catch and foolish virgins among the bridal party. The Ecclesia does not equal the Elect:

> The Church perfected in heaven is the jewel God stooped to covet, but to purchase it He must buy the whole field in which it is buried, and the treasure must be hid until the purchase is completed. We do not know why God values the outward and the earthly as well as the inward and the spiritual; we only know that He does so, because He created us in His Image, because in our image He redeemed us. We should not have designed such a Church as His? Perhaps not, but then, should we have designed such a world as His? The Church, if she is His, must bear the pinxit of the Creator in her very imperfections.[2]

[2] Knox, "Organized Church", p. 86.

Much of Jesus' teaching is directed not to the crowds but to his disciples. In fact, it is extraordinary how much time he devotes to the formation of this inner circle: "All through his ministry his thoughts seem to be centered on their ministry, which is to be the posthumous continuation of his own" (*BC,* 124). He is always at pains to impress them with a sense of their calling. They are fishers of men, salt of the earth, light for the world; they are the scattered reapers of his harvest, the new bottles chosen to receive his new wine (*BC,* 124).

Turning to the Acts of the Apostles, Knox finds a self-contained and self-conscious body that seems able to face every situation with a "wonderful sureness of touch": choosing a new Apostle, designating deacons, holding a Council, all on its own responsibility (*BC,* 125). He observes:

> Is it credible that this peaceful, orderly development should not have been in line with the expressed intention of their Founder? Is it not plain that the Acts form a history spiritually continuous with the Gospels; and that the continuity of a single organized body, the Christian Church, which can easily be traced to the period of the Acts, is thus traceable to our Lord himself? (*BC,* 126).

Finally, he notes the images of the Church used by Paul, which speak of her corporate, visible, growing nature: bride, body, and building (*PS,* 514–18).

The "Marks" of the Church

"This good wine Christ has given us—it is only natural, in an imperfect world, that there should be some confusion about the labels" (*US,* 231). Once it has been decided that Christ founded a Church, the question is, "Which Church?" Because of his conviction that this Church is a visible society, Knox holds that the four notes or "marks" of the Church professed in the Nicene Creed offer signposts pointing the way to the Church of Christ.

ONE

To say that the Catholic Church is One holds a double significance for Knox: it means she is both unique and indivisible. There is only one Church of Christ, and this Church can never be divided:

> The whole issue depends upon your answer to the question, "What happens when there is a schism in the Christian body? What is left?" If you answer "Two Churches" or "Two divided parts of the Church", then you are not a Catholic. If you say "One Church and one sect," then you are in agreement with Catholic Christendom.[3]

Far from destroying the unity of the Church, the vicissitudes of history have augmented it. The inquirer into the history of the Catholic Church will find that

> its unity is not that of a synthetic construction, but that of a statue, gradually hewed into more and more of firmness, of explicitness, of hard outline, and that if the conception of a later age differed from that of a former one it differed not by being out of harmony with it, but by having achieved fuller determination.[4]

For Orthodox and Protestant Christians, "undivided Christendom is a memory in the past, a figment in the present, a

[3] Ronald Knox, *The Church on Earth* (London: Burns Oates and Washbourne, 1929), p. 18.

[4] Ronald Knox, introduction to *God and the Supernatural: A Catholic Statement of the Christian Faith*, ed. Father Cuthbert (London: Longmans, Green, 1920), p. 13.

dream of the future; not a living reality as it is for us" (*BC,* 119).

It would be difficult to find a clearer articulation of the Roman Catholic understanding of unity as it was envisioned in the first half of the twentieth century. Knox recognizes, however, that there is not perfect unity in the Catholic Church: wars between Catholic countries, competition between religious orders, Popes and Antipopes all remind us how imperfect the unity of the Church is.

HOLY

This note is the most elusive. How can holiness be claimed as a mark of the Catholic Church when men of outstanding sanctity are encountered in other religions? How can this claim be squared with a body that has scandalized the world with corrupt Popes, the Inquisition, and the Saint Bartholomew's Day Massacre?

Knox does not dodge the fact of "unholiness" in the Church; he admits that it is probably less safe to leave one's umbrella at the door of a Catholic church than at the door of a Methodist one (*US,* 61). In a sense, this unholiness is a compliment; it means that a Catholic does not cease to be a Catholic because he is a rogue; he knows what is right even when he is doing what is wrong.

Knox also recognizes that the Catholic Church enjoys no monopoly on virtue; heroic Christianity is present in every denomination. What then does this mark mean? Knox mentions the stock apologetic response—the Catholic claim to holiness is proved by the continuance of miracles and the existence of religious orders. He then adds:

> I've no quarrel with that explanation, but I think you can put the thing more simply in this way—Christians of any other

denomination, if they describe that denomination as "holy" at all (which they very seldom do), are referring in fact to the individual holiness of its members. Whereas when we talk about the Holy Catholic Church we aren't thinking, precisely, of the holiness of its members. We think of the Church as sanctifying its members, rather than being sanctified by its members (*US*, 233).

Through her sacraments, her liturgy, her art, and her organizations, the Catholic Church makes her people holy.

Sanctity is an elusive quality; very often God's candidate is not the world's, and the floodlight will be trained on some obscure niche in a convent or within the walls of a prison (*OS*, 150). The Catholic Church is "holy" because she generates holiness. But Knox tells his hearers that individual holiness, or the lack of it, has apologetic impact. Great saints and notorious criminals constitute two ends of the spectrum. We ordinary Catholics are somewhere in the middle, and it is to us that most people will look for a sign of the Church's power to sanctify. He warns against a temptation to mediocrity:

Our terrible second-ratedness, our determination to get to heaven as cheaply as possible, the mechanical way in which we accept our religious duties, our habit of thinking about every problem of conduct in terms of sin and hell, when we ought to be thinking much more about generosity in our treatment of God (*US*, 234).

CATHOLIC

The worldwide organization of Roman Catholicism is an obvious fact. But "catholicity" means far more than that for Knox: "To be a Catholic does obliterate, instead of emphasizing, the sense of strangeness which you and I have when we meet a foreigner" (*US*, 234). The Catholic Church is

not a national church; being born an Englishman may give
one the right to belong to the Church of England; being
born a man gives one the right to belong to the Church
of Rome.[5] Knox underscores the meaning of this aspect of
catholicity in a sermon on the Eucharist preached during
the Second World War:

> The Blessed Sacrament, the Jerusalem of our souls, stands
> apart from and above all the ebb and flow of world-politics,
> its citizenship a common fellowship between us and those
> who are estranged from us, those who at the moment are our
> enemies. Our friends yesterday, our friends tomorrow—in
> the timeless existence to which that altar introduces us, they
> are our friends today (*PS*, 210).

The Church is also catholic in the variety of people she
attracts. She is not a foolish mother who tries to make her
children like everything that she likes; she seeks to meet the
individual needs and desires of each (*US*, 436–37). This variety of tastes within the Church is bound to cause a certain
amount of friction. Knox tells a possible convert that it is
better to join the Church knowing that you hate a dozen
things about her day-to-day life rather than in "a love-sick
admiration of everything and anything she sanctions" (*OR*,
143).

He also admits that this "catholicity" is not perfect. There
is often a suspicion regarding new ways of doing things. The
Roman Church is catholic in the geographical sense; he wonders, is she also catholic in the field of ideas? (*US*, 235).

Another aspect of her catholicity is temporal: the Church
embraces not only space but time. Those who have gone
before are still a real part of the Church. The Church Tri-

---

[5] Ronald Knox, *Anglican Cobwebs* (London: Sheed and Ward, 1928), p. 23.

umphant, the Church Suffering, the Church Militant are all part of one body; or as Knox described it to the girls at Aldenham: "All Saints, All Souls, All Sorts" (*CSM,* 197). Knox reminds them that we can help the deceased in purgatory, and in turn rely on the saints, the "cloud of witnesses", described in the twelfth chapter of the Letter to the Hebrews, which constitute our "rooting section":

> And are they content with watching? Do they simply look on, and wonder which side will win? Is that the common attitude of spectators, when they watch an athletic contest? That is not my memory of the days, nearer thirty years ago than I care to think, when I used to watch the football matches at the Aston Villa ground. My memory is rather of a small boy, wearing a claret-and-light-blue favour, who stood up on a seat and booed the referee. They are witnesses of our race, these martyrs of ours, but something more than witnesses, partisans who can cheer us to victory with the breath of their applause (*OS,* 107).

APOSTOLIC

To speak about the Church as "catholic" and "apostolic" seems to set up a paradox: the Church is described as universal in scope, yet tied to the doctrine handed down centuries ago in an obscure Roman province. The essence of apostolicity for Knox is the faithful handing on of a message (*US,* 236). The message is apostolic, and to the extent that a community professes the faith preached by the first Apostles, to that extent it is apostolic. To the charge that Catholics do not really hold this faith, Knox retorts:

> Why on earth the world supposes that we go on repeating to one another and to the general public a series of statements in which we do not believe ourselves, I for one could never

discover. It must, surely, be some monstrous perversion of
the intellect which enables three hundred millions of people
to recite a common creed Sunday by Sunday and wink at one
another as they do so! (*PS,* 183).

But the Catholic Church is not only apostolic in the content of her faith, she is also apostolic in the mission of her
leaders. It is not enough, in the New Testament, to be called;
one must also be sent. Knox maintains that the ministers of
other Christian denominations may be called, but they have
not been sent; they cannot trace their mandate back to those
commissioned by our Lord himself. As an Anglican priest,
Knox was disturbed by the question, "Matthew Parker had
sent me; who sent Matthew Parker?"[6] He felt the only historically honest answer was "Queen Elizabeth". Whether
his orders were valid or not, he came to believe that they
were not an expression of the commission of Christ passed
on by his Apostles.[7]

"Apostolic" can refer to the content of the faith and to
the body professing it. In a letter written to Laurence Eyres
a few years after his own conversion, Knox discussed the
relative value of these two meanings:

> I think your real issue . . . is this: am I to find out what is the
> *fides* and thus be in a position to label the people *fideles* or not
> at my discretion? Or am I to find out who are the *fides*, and
> learn my *fides* from them? If the former, then you will have
> to thresh out every possible article of belief in light of 3 or
> 4 different competing systems of religion. If the latter, then
> you must find a body of Christians which, without first in-

[6] Matthew Parker (1504–1575) was the first Archbishop of Canterbury in
the reign of Queen Elizabeth I.
[7] Ronald Knox, "Why I Am a Catholic", in *Why I am a Catholic*, ed. Hilaire Belloc et al. (New York: Macmillan, 1952), pp. 62–63.

specting its beliefs, you can see to be descended straight from
the Apostles. At least, that was my conclusion, and I could
find no Body (in that sense) except the Roman Church.[8]

Catholics and Non-Catholics

It is a violation of simplicity, when you allow partisanship
to run away with your sympathies, unable to find fault with
anybody who belongs to your crowd, unable to find any good
motives in people who belong to the other crowd. This is a
temptation which is very real to us Catholics. Our sympathies
are so strongly engaged, we are so widely at variance with
most of our fellow countrymen, that we are prone to bias.
We try to simplify history, we try to simplify politics, by
making them all black and white, all heroes and villains; and
in doing that we only unsimplify ourselves (*OS,* 94).

The man who spoke those words to Catholic undergraduates in 1954 was reflecting on his own experience. Ronald
Knox yielded at times to the temptation of partisanship. This
is partly due to his own conversion and partly to the attitude
of the Catholic Church herself in the first half of the twentieth century. Nothing arouses more antagonism against the
Catholic Church, Knox notes, than her exclusiveness (*BC,*
195). He sums up a chapter in *The Belief of Catholics* on
"Catholics and Those Outside":

In a word, the unity of the Church has hard edges. Of this
our Protestant ancestors did not complain; they had their hard
edges too. Our generation, suckled on the milk of nineteenth-
century liberalism, still hankers after cloudy formulas and in-
definite compromise (*BC,* 204).

[8] Ronald Knox to Laurence Eyres, Aug. 30, 1920, in "Letters from R. A.
Knox to L. E. Eyres", ed. L. E. Eyres, typescript, University of London, p.
46.

Beneath Knox' search for authority in religion lies a deeper quest: he is seeking salvation. Membership in the Church is more than a matter of party spirit for him. If at times he is stern in his views of other denominations, this tendency must be seen against the background of the question of our eternal destiny. The world finds the Christian insistence on salvation or damnation annoying:

> You know what it's like if seven people are sitting in a railway-carriage on a rather cold day, with both windows up and all the heating on and a really good fug to sit in; and then at some way-side station an eighth traveler gets in who opens the window to look out and say good-bye to his wife and then doesn't quite pull it up to the top, so that some of the cold air gets in. That is how the world feels about the Christian Church, with her talk of heaven and hell (*CSM,* 87).

So the question of joining the Catholic Church may be a matter of eternal life or death.

Knox uses the parable of the treasure in the field to illustrate the mysterious element of salvation:

> The man who buys the field buys the field for the sake of the treasure; redeems all mankind in order that he may save —some. No, there is no truce with Jansenism; he bought the whole field, died for the sins of the whole world, yet it is not the whole world that his death will profit. In the unfathomable fore-knowledge of Almighty God some souls shine out like gold, though they were still buried and sunk in earthly defilement. . . . For their sakes Jesus Christ made the world his own possession at the price of his precious blood. . . . And, having found the treasure, notice that the man hides it again; only he knows the secret of the *cache.* Only God fore-knows the souls that are his; it is not for us to say this man is saved, or that lost. Only the shortest of the parables, only a single verse of the Gospel, and here is Calvin

as well as Jansen refuted from the lips of Incarnate Truth (*PS*, 88).

"It is not for us to say this man is saved, or that lost." Membership in the Church does not guarantee eternal life. Does refusal of membership exclude one from eternal life?

> It would be hard to prove from our Lord's own words that he meant otherwise; the whole weight of the texts emphasizes the momentous importance of welcoming the apostolic testimony.[9]

Yet this crucial challenge in the preaching of Jesus must be tempered with two other truths: people do not go to hell except through their own fault (*US*, 241), and God does not deny his aid to anyone who does their best (*US*, 243). *Extra Ecclesiam nulla salus?* This is one of the most difficult of Christian questions. To affirm it would seem to limit God's mercy to certain human, and imperfect, channels. To deny it would seem to remove the urgency of the Kingdom preached by Jesus, reducing one's response to a matter of personal taste.

In dealing with this question, Knox highlights the "hard edges" of Catholic unity. Signs of a thaw in this regard may be found in his later writings. For example, in the conference concluding this chapter he points out that Catholicism has many things in common with other religions and that the common ground between Rome and other Christian bodies is extensive.[10]

---

[9] Knox, "Why I Am a Catholic", p. 57.
[10] Ronald Knox, "The Brute Fact of Christianity", unpublished conference, typescript, 1954, Knox Papers, Mells, Somerset; see pp. 235–43 of this book.

The Teaching Church

In his ministry, Jesus taught with authority, and the response to his invitation had its repercussions in the eternal destiny of his hearers. This ministry was only the beginning of a campaign intended by Christ to spread out to the whole world down through the ages. Knox sees the Catholic Church as the visible community founded by Christ to prolong his saving mission.

How could Jesus extend his revelation beyond his lifetime? Knox sees two possible vehicles: a written record or a living witness. He argues that Jesus did not choose to perpetuate his revelation primarily by means of a written record, because (1) Jesus himself never left any writings behind; (2) a written record demands interpretation, and thus a living witness; (3) the early Church possessed the "Gospel" for years before committing her faith to writing. Accordingly,

> the Christian revelation was not enshrined in a Book; it was enshrined in a Life. . . . The safeguarding of revelation depended therefore, upon a set of first-hand witnesses, who were called apostles, and next to them upon "elders," whose memory would go furthest back. The Church was thus a teaching Church in its earliest beginnings, religious certitude was based upon a set of living memories; and those memories were perpetuated in the first instance by tradition.[11]

This reliance on living witnesses creates another problem: What kind of guarantee is there that this testimony is true? In response to this question, Knox points to the conviction found in the Church from primitive times that she enjoys the constant guidance of her risen Lord, which protects her

[11] Knox, *The Church on Earth*, p. 32.

from serious doctrinal error. Such guidance is essential to the conditions of revelation and to the integrity of his revelation by protecting his Church from error. From this conviction, it follows that

> intellectually speaking, the position of one who "submits to the Church" is that of one who has reached a satisfactory induction—namely, that the Church is infallibly guided into all truth—and can infer from it, by a simple process of deduction, the truth of the various doctrines which she teaches. He does not measure the veracity of the Church by the plausibility of her tenets; he measures the plausibility of her tenets by the conviction he has already formed of her veracity. Thus, and thus only can the human intellect reasonably accept statements which (although they cannot be disproved) cannot be proved by human reason alone (*BC*, 144).

When considering Knox' understanding of the apostolicity of the Church, we saw that he applies the word in a double sense: it refers both to the witnesses and to the content of the tradition. In one unpublished conference, he addresses the distinction between the *Ecclesia docens* and the *Ecclesia discens*—the "Teaching Church" and the "Learning Church". He maintains that these are not two parts of the Church: the whole Church is both. The whole Church bears witness to the apostolic faith, and the *consensus fidelium* is one of the signs that a doctrine is authentically Catholic.[12]

That being said, within the community, her leaders, as the successors to the Apostles, have a special charism to teach, and it is in this context that Ronald Knox speaks of bishops, Ecumenical Councils, and the Pope. He has little to

---

[12] Ronald Knox, "The Teaching Church", unpublished typescript, n.d., Knox Papers, Mells, Somerset. Text may be found in Milton Walsh, *Ronald Knox as Apologist* (S.T.D. diss., Gregorian University, Rome, 1985), pp. 409–20.

say on the teaching office of bishops. They are recognized channels of the apostolic tradition from the earliest days of the Church;[13] they are the spokesmen of the faith of their local churches. Knox' reticence on this point should not be attributed to a desire to denigrate episcopal teaching authority. It is partly due to the tendency in Catholic thought in his time to emphasize the papal magisterium, and partly to the fact that Anglicans and Roman Catholics were in general agreement on the teaching role of the bishop; this did not have to be defended so vigorously. For example, Knox alludes to the teaching office of bishops as a "given" when discussing the papacy with Arnold Lunn:

> I am rather sorry you do not want to argue more about the meaning of the Petrine texts. Your modest claim that the three texts do not constitute a "legal charter" for the Papacy might surely be paralleled by saying that the words "As the Father hath sent me, even so I send you . . . whosoever sins ye remit," etc., etc., are not a *legal charter* for the episcopate. In both cases, you have to read the texts in the light of what actually followed as a matter of history; the tradition that the apostolic ministry is continued by bishops, the tradition that the Bishop of Rome succeeds to the pre-eminent position of Peter (*Dif,* 123).

The presence of Holy Spirit protecting the Church from error does not short-circuit human nature; disputes are bound to arise, even among bishops. How are these to be settled? One course followed by the Church has been to gather the world's bishops in an Ecumenical Council. Some of these bishops may be theologians, but their primary function at such a Council is to bear witness to the faith of their communities:

[13] Knox, "Why I Am a Catholic", p. 65.

In that Council [Vatican I] as in all ecumenical councils, the bishops were present primarily in order that each might testify what was the tradition of Catholic antiquity preserved in their own see. They might be called upon to express opinions; to express an opinion, for example, whether it was opportune, at that moment, to define the Infallibility of the Roman Pontiff as an article of Catholic Faith. But in the first instance, they were expected not to contribute opinions, but to give voice to a testimony. . . . The Fathers of the Vatican Council, though many of them held the opinion that it was not a suitable moment for defining Papal Infallibility, all agreed that the infallibility of the Pope was part of the doctrine commonly received in their sees, doctrine which had been handed down to them by their predecessors (*OS,* 178).

When the bishops bear witness to their faith, one of them holds a unique position:

The tradition of those cities, like Ephesus, where apostles took up their headquarters, are particularly valuable, because there the tradition is likely to have survived in its purest form. But Rome stands altogether by itself; for Rome has the tradition of that apostle who was commanded to "confirm his brethren." Its Bishop has a tradition of doctrine which is, by divine guarantee, immune from error as is the general tradition of doctrine collectively given to the Church (*Dif,* 126).

The Bishop of Rome is the final arbiter of the Church, and as such must possess in some way the charism of infallibility. The only alternative arbiter would be an Ecumenical Council, but this idea suggests to Knox a vicious circle. There is no way to decide which councils are ecumenical except by saying that those councils were ecumenical that were ratified by the Pope (*US,* 94). In fact, he suggests that the main function of the papacy in regard to doctrine is not to define infallible truths but to declare which councils are genuine

(*OR*, 69). Infallible papal statements are rare; the purpose of the decree of papal infallibility was to decide a point of principle, not to establish a practice. That principle is the independence of the Roman Church's inerrancy (*Dif*, 128).

The doctrine of papal infallibility is so misunderstood, even by Catholics, that Knox strives to "demythologize" it. It is not a matter of private inspiration, or consulting a kind of "Urim and Thummim" in the Vatican:

> Every Pope, in every decision, makes up his mind as best he can as to the true doctrine of the Church, using every effort to consider the full history of Catholic tradition on the subject. He makes up his mind as anybody else does; the difference is that the Pope, in certain circumstances, is providentially directed so that he makes up his mind right (*Dif*, 124).

Nor should its limits be overextended. Knox told his students at Oxford of a fellow Anglican in his student days who was so convinced of the infallibility of the Pope that no Anglican bishop would ordain him; and he was told by the Catholic chaplain that he could not become a Catholic because he wouldn't leave any room for faith in his system (*US*, 253).

Unlike some English converts, Knox was not "Romanized" by becoming a Catholic. In fact, he allowed many years to pass after his conversion before he returned to Rome, observing that "he who travels in the barque of St Peter had better not look too closely into the engine room."[14] (On the occasion of that visit, he had a private audience with Pope Pius XII; they discussed the Loch Ness Monster.) He was always sensitive to how Catholicism appeared to his countrymen, and in spite of his occasional sallies against other

[14] Penelope Fitzgerald, *The Knox Brothers* (London: Macmillan, 1977), p. 258.

denominations, he tried to be mindful of their impression of the Catholic Church. An interesting example of this may be found in a letter written by Knox to Douglas Woodruff, who had asked him to translate the Apostolic Constitution *Munificentissimus Deus*, proclaiming the dogma of Our Lady's Assumption:

> But I have the text, and will make a start on it this evening. Meanwhile, will you perpend whether you really want to have a good translation, or whether it wouldn't be better to have one so dull that nobody will read it? You see, the non-Cath's simply CANNOT understand what we mean by "tradition"; to them it only means a catena of quotations from the first six centuries. And the Encyclical only starts with St Germanus and St John Damson, who are both 7th–8th centuries; then it goes on to St Thomas and St Francis of Sales and all manner of moderns. Everybody outside the Church will say at once, "There! What did we tell you? It isn't primitive." People will read the document, expecting to find it a careful piece of apologetics, and will only find (from their point of view) a piece of flamboyant piety.[15]

Finally, in his presentation of the papacy, Knox portrays it as more than an organ of magisterial teaching:

> Did it never occur to you that we call the Pope the Holy Father because we think of him as our father? That the unity of the Church is not the unity of a machine but the unity of a great family? That our obedience to the Holy Father in that very limited range of affairs in which he demands our obedience is not that of a workman towards the foreman who will sack him if he doesn't work, but it is that of children towards their father—each eager to outdo the others in showing affection; each eager to outstrip the others in anticipating his slightest

[15] Ronald Knox to Douglas Woodruff, Nov. 22, 1950, among Knox' papers, Mells, Somerset.

wish? That we obey him in effect not because we fear him as the doorkeeper of heaven, but because we love him as the shepherd of Christians, of Christ's flock? (*US,* 379)

The Catholic Church is apostolic not only in the sense that her representatives are the legitimate successors to the Apostles but also because the content of her faith is apostolic. Is this content a static body of truths or is it something that develops? Some would hold that it is fixed and accuse the Catholic Church of adding to the apostolic faith. Others, following the second line of thought, would dismiss the Catholic Church as "anachronistic" for continuing to cling to outdated doctrines.

Knox holds that both understandings have some merit: while the core of faith is fixed, its meaning becomes clearer with the passage of time. He uses the analogy of case law. Suppose, he says, there is a law against carrying a weapon. Someone is arrested for carrying a walking stick; a jury must decide if this is a violation of the law. Another person is arrested for carrying a carving knife; again a decision must be made. The law has remained the same, but its meaning has become clearer (*US,* 88–89). Jesus gave his followers the marrow of Christian theology and left it for later generations to work out its implications: "If you'd asked St Peter, for example, what was meant by the Hypostatic Union, he would probably have said, 'You can search me'" (*CSM,* 191).

This development and clarification often comes about when a truth is challenged. A theologian attempts to explain a Christian mystery more closely. If this explanation does not do justice to the full reality of the Christian faith, other theologians respond: "The fine flower of Christian scholarship is fertilized, you may say, by the decaying corpse of false doctrine" (*OS,* 35). At times, the leadership of the

Church will make an authoritative statement in a theological dispute:

> One hears that tramps have a special sign which they chalk up on the walls of a house which means, "No good trying here; you won't get anything out of that". . . . In the same sort of way, the Church, who has centuries of experience behind her, chalks up, as it were, on certain lines of theological speculation, "No good trying here, you won't get anything out of that" (*US,* 97).

Such definitions produce a clearer expression of the apostolic faith. But Knox also notes that they can create a polemical atmosphere, as happened after the Council of Trent. The whole strength of the Church was dedicated to securing the Catholic position against attack: "Her philosophers became controversialists, her theologians propagandists, her preachers missionaries" (*PS,* 92).

The Life of the Church

Throughout this chapter, it has been seen how Knox attempts to depict persuasively the contours of Catholicism. Such an exercise is the natural field of apologetics; yet the picture is incomplete. Knox does seek to describe the shape and structure of the Catholic Church, more often than not to the curious (not to say perplexed) outsider. But he also wishes to present something of what it feels like to *be* a Catholic, how the Church appears from the inside. He concludes his essay "Why I am a Catholic" with an examination of his feelings since his conversion, "lest it be supposed that the consolations of the Catholic life are merely an exercise in logic".[16] The second half of *The Belief of Catholics* is

---

[16] Knox, "Why I Am a Catholic", p. 74.

devoted to "The Air Catholics Breathe", "The Truths Catholics Hold", "The Rules Catholics Acknowledge", "The Strength Catholics Receive", and "The Ambitions Catholics Honour".

A good summary of these "views from within" can be found in a sermon preached by Knox on the parable of the Good Samaritan. Following the imagery of the Fathers, he sees the inn as a symbol of the Church:

> Three things above all we shall look for in the inn—refreshment, good company, and repose. What refreshment this inn gives us, as we feed upon the body and blood of Christ! What company, as we are knitted together in its holy fellowship with all God's chosen people in this world and beyond—our boon companions at the divine altar! What rest for sin-worn consciences, when scruples and doubts and fears are lulled by the murmur of absolution, and we can draw free, deep breath once more! We are all convalescents, recovering by degrees from the terrible blow sin dealt to us, building ourselves up and making the most of our time till the good Physician gives us our discharge and we are fit to travel safely home (*PS,* 84).

In the Catholic Church, Ronald Knox had found a solid authority for his faith, but he had found much more: refreshment, good company, and healing. And he hoped his readers would find them, too.

THE BRUTE FACT OF CHRISTIANITY

When I came down last term, I was talking about the position of the Jewish people in history, and suggesting that in some ways it is a quite unique phenomenon. And this morning I have got to talk about another phenomenon, a parallel phenomenon, unique in its turn—I mean the position of the Christian Church in history. The brute fact of Christianity; we are going to talk about that, the mere impact on the world of ideas and institutions which owe their inspiration to our Lord Jesus Christ; not by way of proving that they are particularly noble or beneficial, but by way of pointing out that they are remarkable; Christianity, whatever way you look at it, is a fact to be reckoned with. Why should that be necessary? For this reason; your conferences this term will be devoted to shewing that the interpretation we put on the events which took place in the first century does hold water. But before we do that, we want to remind ourselves that the enquiry is worth making. Or rather, not to remind ourselves; of course it interests us. But we shall be coming across people who are not prepared to make it, simply because the subject doesn't seem to them significant. So this morning we are going to prepare the way by reflecting that the subject *is* significant. The impact of Christianity on the world is not just one of those things; it is a phenomenon which ought to be intriguing to the imagination.

All the more necessary, because nowadays some people have developed a rather up-stage habit of talking about the Christian religion as if it were merely a phase through which

Ronald Knox, "The Brute Fact of Christianity", unpublished conference, typescript, 1954, Knox Papers, Mells. First delivered at the Catholic Chaplaincy, Oxford University in 1954.

the world has been passing, a phase which it has nearly out-
grown; they have invented, to annoy us, the word "post-
Christian". Arnold Toynbee has had a good deal to do with
that. I am not setting out to prove that any of his theses are
untrue, because when you cut up history into such enor-
mous slabs, proof and disproof in the strict sense become
impossible. It will be known a hundred years hence how
wrong the rest of us were; it will take at least a thousand
years to shew how wrong Arnold Toynbee was. Let them
have it their own way; let us admit the possibility in the
abstract, that Christianity is all but played out; will soon
be as dead as Mithras. Perhaps, in a thousand years' time,
town-planners will be appealing for its preservation, with
that passionate tenderness which Englishmen always shew
for the extinct. Even if we could believe that, I would still
claim that Christianity is not just one of those things, it is a
portrait; and the historian will not have done his duty until
he has explained to us how it came to catch on so suddenly,
to bite so deep, to arouse so much debate; why men so loved
and hated it, so laboured to abolish it.

Two things I must say by way of preliminary. We shall be
comparing the Christian religion all the time with the other
religions of the world, but only by inference. It is not unique
in every point, and sometimes what we shall be saying about
it could equally be said of Mahommedamism, [*sic*] perhaps,
or of Buddhism. It is only the total effect that we are considering. And again, Christianity presents itself to the world,
more's the pity, under a multitude of different forms; and
often what you say about it is true of one denomination,
but not of another. I want it to be understood, then, that I
am thinking particularly of that body of Christians which is
in visible communion with the Holy See. Much of what I
say will be true of other denominations, but not all of it; no

matter. Catholicism is Christianity at its most challenging; Christianity in the raw.

And now let me shoot at you a whole series of considerations on this subject, which I shall have no time to substantiate or even to explain fully. First, Christianity is one of the mystery religions, and at the same time (if I may put it in that way) one of the history religions. Not only Mithraism but a whole lot of other more or less secret cults were fashionable in the world of the first century, but they were quite unrelated to fact. They didn't try to prove their assertions; they linked themselves with the mythology of a remote and shadowy past. What gave them their appeal was that they offered an escape from materialism. Christianity also offered an escape from materialism, but it linked itself with the name of a historical Person, the contemporary of its first converts. To find salvation, you must believe on the name of somebody who died only yesterday, as real as Cicero.

Second, Christianity was at once a development of something already in existence, and a complete breakaway from it. In a sense it was Judaism carried to its logical conclusion; in a sense it was Judaism turned inside out. Its Apostles made no statement which they were not prepared to justify, at least remotely, by quotations from the Old Testament; and at the same time the intense nationalism which breathes in every line of the Old Testament was flung to the winds. It was at once the end of a chapter and the beginning of a new one; the answer to a riddle, and the propounding of a fresh riddle; it derived strength from the stock on to which it was grafted, and at the same time the freedom of its own growth was not hampered by the connexion.

Third, it took over, and assimilated, just so much of heathen symbolism as genuinely interpreted the religious aspirations of the human mind. If a pagan, looking at some early representation of the Good Shepherd in the twilight of the catacombs, exclaimed, "Why, that's Orpheus", the Christian reply wasn't, "No, nothing of the kind; that's the Good Shepherd". The Christian reply was, "Of course it's Orpheus; that's what Orpheus was; he was a type, dimly foreseen by muddled heathen minds, of our Christ; he was represented as going down to the world beneath, just as our Christ, after his Passion, went down to the world beneath". And so on. Mark you, that process of baptizing, instead of obliterating, the relics of paganism didn't always pass without criticism. Clement of Alexandria in the third century was frowned upon for trying to work too much of the old religion into his Christian scheme; and there was the same trouble fifteen centuries later, when the Jesuits started trying to convert China in pig-tails. There is always the fear that accommodation will go too far; but always the Catholic instinct, in defiance of Puritanism, has been that natural religion can be made to dove-tail into the supernatural.

Fourth, Christianity is at once the religion of a church and the religion of a book. If any religious movement is to survive, seriously, the life-time of its founder, it must have some guarantee of continuity. That will mean, either a set of trustees, pledged to carry out, age after age, the intentions of the founder; or else a written code, treated as sacrosanct and therefore remaining unaltered. The continuity of the Christian Church is presented in both ways, by a written record and by an unbroken tradition. This is true of other religions, but it is doubtful whether any other religion has clung so obstinately to a belief in both safeguards at once. The importance of this could easily be shewn by tracing the history of certain non-Catholic movements, but we must not allow ourselves to spend time over that.

Fifth, the Christian religion is not, what most religions are, the reflection, the off-print, of one particular civilization or one particular part of the world's surface. That, of course, is at first sight a controversial statement. Years ago, Mr Belloc produced a rather misleading slogan, "Europe is the Faith, and the Faith is Europe". People are coming to talk nowadays as if that were true; as if Christianity were only a statement in spiritual terms of the values cherished by what we vaguely call "The West". But if that is, at the moment, geographically true, it is not historically true. Until the rise of Mohammedanism, the gospel, cradled in a country which belongs essentially to the east, spread eastwards as well as westwards by what seemed a quite natural process. Only when Mohammedanism, itself a kind of Christian heresy, cut off the east from the west, was that process suspended. Meanwhile, you would have supposed that Christian religion expressed the values cherished by the Roman-Greek empire of the first centuries. Yet it survived the death of that empire, and set its seal upon the new order which emerged after the barbarian invasions. The attempt to capture Christianity and make it run in harness with the ideals of one particular empire, one particular form of culture, is constantly being made, but always it breaks the bonds in which we seek to imprison it.

Sixth, the Christian religion is both this-worldly and other-worldly. A religion may tend to lavish all its energies upon turning the world into a better place, teaching men to fit into their surroundings, and making good citizens of them, good neighbours of them. Or it may encourage us to bestow all our attention upon the next life, paying little heed to what happens in this; its tendency may be to lift men above this world, rather than fit him into it. In ancient Greece you see the two religions at work side by side, the Olympian religion which regulated man's place in the state, and the underworld religion of the mysteries which gave him, however faintly, the hope of a hereafter. Most of our Lord's teaching in the gospels is, you may say, of the other-worldly type, and the whole tradition of Christian asceticism has been to treat this world as dust and ashes, not worth bothering about. And yet Christianity, wherever it has been true to its own genius, has thrown itself into the service of the poor and the sick, has tried to iron out the hardships of this life. Mary and Martha are sisters.

Seventh, the Christian religion absorbs human learning and speculation. It does not, like the old religions of Greece and Rome, adopt a policy of appeasement, and so let religion thin out into mere philosophy. Nor, like Islam ever since the Middle Ages, does it turn its back on human learning and frown on human speculation, shutting itself up in an intransigent fundamentalism. Oh, to be sure, there has been plenty of tension in the past; St Thomas was very nearly treated as a heretic because he was securing a come-back for Aristotle; and there are tensions still. But always the Church refuses what seems to be the easiest path, that of deciding that there are two different kinds of truth, one philosophical and one theological; that way, she knows, madness lies.

Eighth, the Christian religion expresses itself in music and the arts, yet will not admit good taste into the highest range of values. The Church has been the mother of the arts, and turns away impatiently from the Puritanism which regards all beauty as a snare. At the same time she will not be captured by mere beauty, or confuse the aesthetic with the moral. Belloc put that point well: "Note you, she is still careless of art or songs, as she has always been. She lays her foundations on something other, which something other our moderns hate. Yet out of that something other came the art and song of the Middle Ages."

Ninth, the Christian religion holds the balance jealously between mysticism and the intellect. Always there will be those who despair of the intellect, and claim that there is no true way to God except an unreasoning aspiration which gives us direct, though obscure, knowledge of him. Always there will be an orthodox reaction against this point of view, Bossuet against Fénelon; how are we to distinguish this mystical approach from sheer illuminism? And always the Church keeps her head. She will not allow us to decry the intellect, and treat it as a mere hewer of wood and drawer of water, built only for practical needs; no, it is a ladder whose top is lost in the unseen. And yet we are to leave the mystic at his prayers; why should we be envious of him if God has shewn him a back-door which we are not allowed to use? Of faith itself, she will not allow us to say either that it is unreasonable, or that it is cold reason. She keeps the balance.

Tenth, the Church holds the balance again between internal and external religion. If the exercise of religion is to be social, it is not possible to do away altogether with external ceremonies, common attitudes of worship, common formulas of prayer. And when she orders us to do this or that, it is the external performance of the act she prescribes; she commands us to go to Mass, she does not command us to enjoy ecstasies of devotion when we get there. Outward signs of reverence which have become so familiar that they have almost ceased to engage our attention, like taking holy water or crossing ourselves at grace—she will have it that there is some value in them, even if they are negligently done. So far you might mistake the Christian religion for one of mere formalism. And yet, how constantly the Church puts us on our guard against mere formalism, insists on the value of our intentions in the sight of God! We are body and spirit, and we are meant to praise God with both parts of our nature; that is her drift.

Eleventh—Christianity combines elasticity with a love of tradition. The human mind tends always towards the rut; and religion, left to itself, will cling to a multitude of ceremonies and observances, whose exact performance is the guarantee of perpetuity; doctrines may be whittled away, as the centuries go on, and ardour of the spirit may cool, but always the thing looks the same, and men's minds are at rest. Exactly the opposite of this is the instinct of the Church. It is the outward accessories that change, with her. What horror and what amusement it caused me, in my Anglican days, to hear of the communion service being celebrated in the evening; what a hideous break with all Catholic precedent! And here we are in 1954, with evening Mass and evening communion already a familiar feature of Catholic worship. It is the inner core of things, the tradition, the spirit, that must be kept alive, the accessories do not matter.

Twelfth, the Christian religion combines authority with liberty. A large subject; you would not expect me to discuss, in two or three minutes, the exact justification of this or that burden which the Catholic Church puts on her members. All I am concerned to point out at the moment is that she does exercise authority, in laying down rules which her members must keep, on pain of forfeiting her privileges; yet she allows, within the framework of those rules, much liberty of conscience. Here too, she will not let go of one half of the truth.

Thirteenth, the Christian religion holds up before us a frighteningly high standard of morals, yet is infinitely tender with the conscience of the sinner. In maintaining that attitude, the Church is visibly in line with the practice of her Master. And, like him, she gives thereby abundant scandal to her enemies. When they are not reproaching her with John the Baptist's asceticism, they are reproaching her for eating with publicans and sinners. And, mark you, it is not that she divides up her children into two groups, as other religions have, expecting a higher standard from one group than from the other. No, she expects the highest from all of us; and all the centuries that have passed over her have brought disappointment, but not despair.

Fourteenth, the Christian religion, though so old, is still young. You will not need to be reminded of the incredible recoveries it has made in the most depressing periods of its history; in the Dark Ages, at the Counter-reformation, after the French Revolution. I am not arguing from these precedents that we are likely to see a revival of religion in our life-time; that is as may be. I only say that the phenomenon is worth observing.

Fifteenth, there is no sign whatever of any religion coming along to replace Christianity. The Christian scheme has so imposed itself on men's minds that that is what they mean, nowadays, by religion; even if they would improve on it, they are still driven to use its formulas. Even the Mau-mau propagandists had to substitute the name of their founder for the holy name in the gospels, just as the propagandists of the Risorgimento got up the portrait of Garibaldi to look like Christ's. No, Christianity is like a great love which cannot be replaced by substitutes. The world has had it; and if, a thousand years hence, it is a world without Christianity, it will be a world without religion.

CONCLUSION

"HAPPY THE MAN WHOSE TREASURE-TROVE IS WISDOM" (Prov 3:13)

At the Requiem Mass for Ronald Knox, Martin D'Arcy preached from this text:

> But the wise man will be learning the lore of former times, the prophets will be his study. Theirs it is to support this unchanging world of God's creation; craftsmanship is their title to live—lending themselves freely and making their study in the law of the most High (Eccl 39:1, 38:39).[1]

His comparison of his friend to the sage of Old Testament literature offers a fitting image with which to conclude this exploration of Ronald Knox as a Catholic apologist.

Knox never held an influential office in the Church, nor did he ever serve in a parochial capacity. He devoted his

---

[1] It is intriguing that this is not Knox' translation, because in the course of the panegyric D'Arcy said it was. The text as I give it is what is found in the *Tablet*, and in Waugh's biography.

It is an *amended* version of Knox' translation. First, the citation given by D'Arcy is Ecclesiasticus 38:39. In fact, he is quoting Ecclesiasticus 39:1 and then 38:39. In a footnote to his translation, Knox said that the last 14 words of chapter 38 really belong with chapter 39; D'Arcy followed this lead, but also reversed the verses.

Secondly, D'Arcy changed a few words: his "craftsmanship is their title to live" in Knox' translation is "they ply their craft and ask for nothing better".

So, Knox' Bible was creating problems to the very end.

245

life to scholarship, and to sharing that scholarship with the general public through sermons, conferences, and books. He was not a professional theologian; his education had formed him in a tradition of liberal arts, and he never sought to specialize in any one branch of learning.

He drew on the commonplace and, like the Wisdom writers, brought his lessons literally "home". We have seen how frequently he tapped human experience in his use of images; it is to this same experience that Wisdom literature appeals. The Old Testament proverbs are model epigrams and metaphors on wisdom or folly in daily life: "Idle hand, empty purse; riches come of hard work" (Prov 10:4); "The mouth, for the just man a life-giving well, for the wicked an arsenal of harm" (Prov 10:11). Pictures from nature describe the destiny of the godless, ". . . thistle-down in the wind, flying spray before the storm, smoke that whirls away in the breeze" (Wis 5:15), and contrarily the path of the just, which "grows ever brighter, like the light of dawn opening out into full day!" (Prov 4:18). The sage recalls his own childhood as he begins to teach: "Time was when I had a father of my own; and when I was but a boy, my mother's darling, in such words as these would he teach me. . ." (Prov 4:3–4). The astute ruler, too, recognizes in his infancy a share in the common lot: "Born was I, and born drew common air . . . swaddled I must be, and cared for, like the rest. Tell me, was ever king had other manner of coming to be?" (Wis 7:3–5). On every side, elements of the everyday teach wisdom —pots and kettles, cold water on parched lips, a rosebush in Jericho, the rushing Jordan at the month of harvest. And this is only right, for when Wisdom himself comes into the village, it is with these same homey images—of lost coins, of lamps, and patched cloaks—that he will teach. Knox followed the example of his Master in clothing his lessons in the imagery of daily life.

By his contemplation of creation and the events of daily life, Knox was able to engage his audience. There is a quality of gentleness and human sympathy in his apologetics giving them an atmosphere of Wisdom, not simply erudition. The majority of his apologetic writings originated as conferences or sermons and were conversational in tone. Knox was not only mindful of what he wanted to say, he was attentive to the nature of his audience. Speaight identifies this as the characteristic element of his preaching:

> What is it, then, that distinguishes these sermons from others which have held their place in the devotional literature of England? It is, I think, a certain note of familiarity . . . whether he was preaching in Westminster Cathedral or the Brompton Oratory, or in some obscure parish church which had called upon him for a special occasion, he was speaking to his own family—and he did not raise his voice. It was not for him to denounce the sins of society or to engage, militantly, in the controversies of the hour. He would exhort, argue, meditate and persuade; he would not thunder or threaten.[2]

His conferences were effective because he interacted with his listeners; he continues to do so with his readers. His ability to address people in their own idiom scandalized a few, who found his approach irreverent. For most, it helped them to realize that "heaven is a good deal nearer to us than we know" (*US,* 340). It was this nearness of heaven that animated his apologetics, leading him to share his faith with humility, insight, and humor.

---

[2] Robert Speaight, *Ronald Knox the Writer* (New York: Sheed and Ward, 1965), p. 234.

Ronald Knox did not live to complete his "new apologetic", but he did write a prayer which he had intended to serve as a preface to the work. Waugh suggests that it stands as an epitaph of his life's work; certainly it captures Ronald Knox as apologist. Knox concludes his "invocation" by addressing God in these words:

> I know well that in your sight every thought of the human mind is full of ignorance and misapprehensions. But some of us—and perhaps, at the roots of our being, all of us—cannot forego that search for truth in which full satisfaction is denied us here. We apprehend that there is no encounter with reality, from without or from within, that does not echo with your foot-fall. We scrutinize the values, and can give no account of them except as a mask of the divine. Something of all these elusive considerations finds a place in my book. And you, who need nobody's service, can use anybody's. So I would ask that, among all the millions of souls you cherish, some few, upon the occasion of reading it, may learn to understand you a little, and to love you much.[3]

---

[3] Ronald Knox, preface to *PGNA,* quoted in Evelyn Waugh, *Monsignor Ronald Knox* (Boston and Toronto: Little, Brown, 1959), p. 335.